MOVING ON BY HIS GRACE

Visionary: Linda Hunt
The Anthology Doctor

Moving on by His Grace
Copyright © 2022 by compiled by Linda Hunt
All rights reserved.

Edited, formatted, and published by
Destiny House Publishing, LLC.
P.O. Box 19774
Detroit, MI 48219
inquiry@destinyhousepublishing.com
www.destinyhousepublishing.com
404.993.0830

Cover by Kingdom Graphic Designs

This work may not be used in any form, or reproduced by any means, in whole or in part, without written permission from the publisher or author. Unless otherwise stated, all scripture is from the King James Version (KJV)

Printed in the United States

ISBN: 978-1-936867-78-3

CONTENTS

Foreword v

Endorsements vii

Introduction: Linda Hunt, Visionary 1

An Enemy Has Done This: Crystal Townsend 5

This Is That: Debra Bernard 25

Moving Forward By Faith: Deborah Glass 37

Transformed By Grace: Geneva James 45

Stuck No More: Valila Wilson 61

From Trauma to Grace: Karen Jaguar 81

FOREWORD
"Moving on by His Grace"
By Apostle Donna Stallings

The kingdom of God is intertwined with powerful endings that answer unsteady and life-shattering beginnings. For instance, while stuck between Pharoah (the past), and a dark sea in front of them (their future), God tells Moses, "Why are you crying out to me? Tell the Israelites to *move one!"* (NIV)

The kingdom of God contains within its DNA genetic information and instructions filled with pre-coded victories that will only allow for kingdom results: our trials to become our triumph; victimized states to convert into victorious endings and poor mindsets to become awakened – through the very onset of the attack. The kingdom DNA declares that "all things will work together for your good" (paraphrased), and you find each author's evidence in every chapter.

Prophetess Linda Hunt has been given a kingdom assignment to open doors and present platforms for those who have been in the background, waiting for the day to be heard and to share the evidence of God's sovereign power in their lives. Together, we have prayed, decreed, and declared that success will envelop her giftings. Through these prayer times, she has birthed "Moving on by His Grace." This book is a jewel, as on its pages are words from those who were silent -- first-time writers who stepped into this space to *tell their story.*

While reading the chapters, one could sense the hurt, shame, and confusion initially, but at the end of every trial, a beautiful grace emerges, propelling the power of freedom while riveting the soul.

Prophetess Linda, congratulations for answering the call to "preach the word" through these unique writings. Preaching on a stage is not the only place to share God's word, and you have located one place of grace. Royal Daughter – which I am honored to call you -- this indeed is your platform that will provide a place for every beautiful freedom writer to declare their victory and love of our Lord and Savior, Jesus Christ.

Well done! Now, *move on* to your next assignment!

ENDORSEMENTS

As I read the story, "Stuck No More", I could relate in so many ways to feel the pain and defeat of the effects of trauma unable to move forward. Yet, as I continued to read, the writer shined a light into darkness and gave clear directions for living a life of abundance!

I really enjoyed the story, "Moving Forward by Faith", it was very encouraging how the author shared her experience in the workforce and handling a very sensitive issue she had to deal with daily.

This story reminds me to continue to step out in faith, regardless of fear and new situations. God's principles will guide me to attain freedom and walk out my vision. Exceptional!

Venetia Lyons

Those who commit to writing, especially those who write books to transform lives, must have the resilience to stay the course! The contributing authors in the anthology, *Moving on by His Grace,* have done just that.

In the midst of some of the most challenging times in our history, we have been presented with an unquestionable shift in how we live, how we move about in a new environment, and how to adjust to the unknown. We have been challenged with a new adaptation to life. In spite of all that has transpired, the writers in this anthology have demonstrated a ravenous faith to move on by the grace of God.

They have moved on by His grace and rose to the challenge through a global pandemic, witnessing racial and social unrest, injustice, deep political polarization, sexism, and global turmoil. The disruptions of 2020 have had a ripple effect, changing and rearranging the religious arena and the way we do church and ministry. Their transformational messages are a testament to the faithfulness of God to His people.

Moving on by His Grace eloquently shares many challenges faced today with a fresh realism, rich theological reflection, and radical faith to keep moving on by His grace. Their faith is seen throughout the pages of their experiences. Faith to move on by His grace was not only verified by their words, but by the power of the Holy Spirit's work in their lives. It is the power of the Holy Spirit that empowers any of us to move on by faith.

Moving on by His Grace provides an opportunity for self-reflection. It is an occasion to look deep within oneself to discover the hidden treasures God has deposited and used as a conduit to transform lives. These authors have demonstrated the biblical truth of Philippians 1:6 "And I am certain that God, who began the good work within you, will continue his work until it is finally finished on the day when Christ Jesus returns." (NLT)

Foreword

"Moving on by His Grace" demonstrates God's gracious love for His children. His love chose us, drew us, saved us, and He is still not done with us. His eternal desire is to bring us into the center of His will according to His divine purpose. Therefore, until we stand before Him, we are to persevere with a heart of obedience, moving on by His grace.

Barba Gentry-Pugh

Moving on by His Grace

INTRODUCTION

Linda Hunt

"**M**oving on by His Grace" became the message God gave me after coming through probably one of the scariest times of my life. I recognized that life is fragile, unpredictable, and yet amazing. I had to depend on Him and another person to care for me during that time. I could not do it alone. I knew that only the grace of God, His divine ability, would bring me through.

I am a survivor. I have survived many things in this life, and maybe you have, too. Unfortunately, in late 2020, I contracted the Covid-19 virus. I was sick for a while before I knew what was wrong with me. I was tired, sluggish, and sleepy. At first, I didn't pay much attention; I kept wearing my mask, thinking, "Oh, I'm just a little tired." I thought it would go away. I just needed more sleep because I am sort of a night owl. But, it didn't go away, so I decided to get tested. I went to my local CVS and did a test. The test came back 3 days later. I tested *positive!* Naturally, I was scared as the numbers at that time were staggering. I did the 14 days of quarantine, and my test returned negative.

My quarantine time was during December when everyone was preparing for the holidays by shopping, buying presents, and cooking. I spent most of my time in bed. I was too weak to even cook. My experience was not as bad as most, but I had no energy. I was totally exhausted. My fever stayed relatively low. I had no real appetite for food, and I thank God for the many families and friends who dropped food on my porch, sent cash apps, and door dashes. I had no energy to do anything but sleep, go to the bathroom, bathe, and go back to bed. One day, my granddaughter, who stayed with me through the entire ordeal, had to help me up from the table after eating soup. I was so weak.

My family was terribly worried about me because people were dying because this virus was just getting started. Hospitals were full, and there were no solutions or answers to what we were dealing with. This was a pandemic, and it was pandemonium! It was not just confined to the United States. This was a worldwide health crisis! I was frightened to even think about going to a hospital because people would go in and not return. Their loved ones were not permitted to visit. It is bad enough to be sick and not have people you love to be a part of your healing process. I had friends I prayed for; they would call me from the hospital in a panic because they were afraid. Some of them were at the point of the doctors giving up on them or putting them on a ventilator. The reason for the ventilator was to assist them in breathing, but it seemed they would not make it back.

I remember nights I would wake up in a panic and think I was not breathing. So I would sit on the side of my bed and pray, "Lord, help me to breathe." This virus was an attack on the breath. The number one symptom was you could not breathe. It also was an attack on your mind. You had to fight the thoughts that would come

Introduction

to your mind thinking you would not survive. That was not my story, and I have a testimony that "You can get through anything."

I want to encourage someone to know, yes, you can get through whatever you are going through. Yes, it may be tough, but you can make it. It took my faith, prayers, and the love of my family and friends who called me, dropped off food, my granddaughter who cared for me, my church family that prayed for me, and others who checked on me. It took the village to nurse me back to health. But that experience made my faith even stronger to know God was with me through that entire ordeal. You will make it no matter what the situation; it has to change. Yes, I said it has to change, and it will.

The internet was one giant obituary at that time, and I was hurt to see so many people I knew and those I didn't know that did not come through the virus. But I did, and you did, too. So, if you are still breathing, that means your work is not done. You still have something to do. You have a purpose, and God has a plan. It's up to you to tap inside yourself to find out what He wants you to do. Do you realize the first thing God gave us was breath? He breathed the breath of life into man, and he became a living soul. Think about it. That virus came to take your breath.

As you read each of these stories, you will see a common thread of these women, some for the first time telling their stories publicly. You will hear each of them describe how they learned through the pain and trauma to move on with their lives by the grace of the Almighty One.

Don't waste another day living outside the purposes and plans of God for your life. Instead, find a book, a coach, a church, a friend, or someone that can help you find out what is your purpose. Again, I admonish you, don't waste another day and don't waste the breath God gave to you as you begin to move on by His grace. He will meet you there.

Know this, *you can get through anything*!

AN ENEMY HAS DONE THIS

Crystal Townsend

"The kingdom of Heaven is like a farmer who planted good seed in his field. But that night, as the workers slept, his enemy came and planted weeds among the wheat, then slipped away. When the crop began to grow and produce grain, the weeds also grew. The farmer's workers went to him and said, "Sir, the field where you planted the good seed is full of weeds! Where did they come from?" "An enemy has done this!" The farmer exclaimed. Matthew 13:24-28a New Living Translation

When I was a little girl, my mother and I lived with her boyfriend and his mother in a two-family flat. I was about 3 years old, but I remember the house, vividly. It had very limited space, so I slept in the bed with my mom and her boyfriend. At night, I remember watching them have intercourse. Only, I didn't know at 3 years old what sex was. I do remember being totally fascinated by the act because I could see that it was enjoyable for them. I watched them moan in pleasure and roll around as if it were fun. My mother's boyfriend had a friend or a male family member that would come around. I cannot remember how this inappropriate relationship started between the man and my 3-year-old self, but we would

French kiss and touch one another inappropriately. Somehow my 3-year-old mind was able to process that this must mean he is my boyfriend. I correlated what I saw my mother and her boyfriend doing and estimated that since this man and I were doing it, it must mean that he is my boyfriend. Nobody ever knew he was molesting me because I didn't know to tell. I actually "enjoyed" having a boyfriend like my mommy.

Over and over throughout my childhood, I was subjected to sexual molestation by grown men whom I thought were my "boyfriends." Once I became a young woman, I still had my virginity, but my innocence had been stolen, only I didn't know it. Grown men became even more aggressive with their intentions. One man attempted to rape me, another car full of men who saw me walking down the street tried to kidnap me and a friend's father propositioned me to have sex with him.

I want you to notice how the enemy had already groomed me for sexual bondage through what's called, sexual imprinting. Sexual imprinting is a process where mating preferences are affected by learning at a young age. The parent is usually the model. I learned to be attracted to grown men because I mimicked my mother's relationship. Furthermore, I learned that it was okay to have a boyfriend. I made certain inferences about what it meant to have a boyfriend based on my mother's relationship. For instance, I knew that if I had a boyfriend, we would have sex with one another. I don't think parents understand that the weight of every choice they make truly affects their children. The enemy is truly walking about as a roaring lion seeking whom he may devour. If you are a parent, be sober and vigilant concerning your children. Of course, we don't raise them from a place of fear. Still, we need to be spiritually astute to guard against "demonic seed." I understand that my mother didn't realize that the enemy was already sowing seeds of sexual perversion in me at 3 years old, by this seemingly innocent relationship she had. But that's just the thing, the enemy always operates incognito. Notice in the above scripture that while men slept, the enemy planted the "bad seeds" The workers were sleeping, which allowed the enemy to propagate his perversion of the field.

Sleeping is an antonym to being alert! In a spiritual sense, being alert means being fully aware and attentive; wide-awake; keen: to have an alert mind. We do this by developing our spiritual senses. How do we develop those senses, you ask? You do it by studying God's Word and practicing the principles therein. Also, spending time in prayer where you are also still and listening. If you do this consistently, your spirit man will increase, and things you wouldn't usually see, hear, or sense will become apparent over time.

The Seed Began to Sprout

As I grew into a young preteen, I loved my daddy. He was my favorite man in the whole world, and I always spent time with him. He treated me like a princess, but other women were always around. I heard his sexual conversations with them. I saw the way he handled them. Unconsciously, I learned that this is how a man who likes a woman treats her. I thought this behavior was normal. Although my daddy treated me with the highest regard, these women were just objects of his desire for a moment. As a young girl, I didn't know how to correctly process what I saw and heard. There was always chaos that ensued because somebody got hurt. Seeing these highs and lows became normal for me to associate with a healthy relationship. Looking back, you never realize how you erroneously process things as a child because you don't have all the tools to do so. You need the adults in your circle to help teach you by modeling correct behavior and having conversations rooted in God's truth. Although I was raised in the church, the standard at home was altogether different. My behavior at home influenced me more than the preaching I heard at church. I did not know that an enemy had done this!

I was a beautiful teenager, but still a virgin. One of my favorite things to do was hang out with my older girl cousin. She was so pretty, and all the guys were after her. We would laugh, go shopping, and talk about everything. She was also a stripper and would tell me about all the "fun" she was having. She had a beautiful figure and would wear very short shorts. I remember this because short shorts became a favorite of mine. These bad seeds were constantly being nurtured by the images and relationships I saw all around me. Yet again, this seed was being fertilized. My subconsciousness was being programmed, and my identity was being solidified. I consistently learned that my worth as a woman was connected to how sexually attractive I am.

Losing My Virginity

By the time I was 16 years old, I was garnering much attention in my neighborhood. I met this guy at school who was the finest I had ever seen. Seriously. He was a senior, had a car, and looked like God literally chiseled him from a piece of bronzed stone. I kid you not. It was the first time in my life that I was attracted to someone and oddly enough, he was attracted to me. My subconscious programming kicked in, and I knew what to do: become sexually attractive. This young man already had a baby on the way. Instead of seeing this as a red flag, it made me feel safe. Do you know why? I was already conditioned in environments that were sexually perverse. It was normal for me at this point. It was so typical that I felt comfort in knowing that he already knew what to do. Things that should be red flags were green lights for me, at this point. After hanging out for a few months, I allowed him to take what innocence I had left. I didn't care that his pregnant girlfriend had caught wind that we had been hanging out and was hurt (because I saw that with my dad). It was normal. That experience awakened something new in me, and for the next 4 years, I continued to be sexually active with whomever I wanted. I remember hurting people deeply and being hurt. Those seeds were now a harvest of bad decisions and left people in pain. What I was doing had become who I was. Sexual perversion became something I identified with.

By the time I was 18, I was pregnant with a child. The father of that child was emotionally & physically abusive. Eventually, this young man went to jail. I lived in a homeless shelter with my infant son. I had a friend in college who was a stripper, and she encouraged me to get my license and come make some money with her. I obliged. This environment once again measured my worth by my sexual attraction, and I thrived. Have you ever noticed how whatever seed is planted at a young age, you seem to constantly find yourself continuing to perpetuate a harvest of darkness? You start noticing the hand of God at work, as well.

Working as a stripper became the precipice for a supernatural move of God in my life. I will say that Abba kept me. I somehow knew not to have any relationships with those men. There's always this glimmer of light, that you can look back on and see that God was with you, even in darkness. There was temptation everywhere I turned, but I refused to devalue myself further by sleeping with any customer from the bar. There were times I would feel my life was in danger; like someone was watching me. I had a boyfriend who would drop me off and pick me up for this very reason.

All of a sudden, I started making less and less money. Men would ask me why was I there? They would say that I looked like I should be someone's wife in church, these were hardened sinners speaking into my life. Abba works like that. He was there the whole time planting good seeds. You may not see a harvest yet, but the seeds Abba plants are powerful. Not one person is born that Abba didn't know before conception. The Word of God declares in Jeremiah 1:4-5 that He knew us before He formed us in our mother's womb and before we were born, He set us apart and appointed us for a purpose. Psalm 139:13 further confirms that God who makes all our delicate, inner parts and has knit us together in our mother's womb. This is why the enemy has shown up to try to circumvent the purpose of God for your life. But God!

Abba was calling me, and I didn't yet recognize it because I didn't know Him. I couldn't identify His voice. All I knew was things were getting weird around me, and my money was drying up. The

Bible says that the way of the transgressor is hard. This hard way is a blessing.

To make things even weirder, I had dreams that a man who looked like death was chasing me at night, but he could never get close enough to kill me. Somehow, I would sense when he was closing in on me and would escape. My mother started having nightmares that I was found raped and strangled. I would get physically sick, but only on my way to work at the strip club.

One night, I fell asleep and dreamed that I was in the strip club's dressing room getting "in character." All of a sudden, people came running and screaming in absolute chaos. They were screeching and yelling out in terror that, "Jesus is here!" Before I could even get up to go see, God himself pulled back the roof of the strip club, and this bright light showed down on me, and I woke up. You know, I was in so much darkness, I still didn't discern that these dreams were Abba's way of communicating with me. I have had them all my life, and I still didn't know that He was talking to me. Even in our sin, Abba pursues us, and there are traces of Him if we really think about it. Where has Abba been trying to get your attention? I pray that every veil, scale, and cover that is over your eyes be removed, That the eyes of your understanding, would be enlightened that you may know what the hope of His calling is and that where you were blind, you would now *see*! In the name of Jesus!

Eventually, I quit stripping and got a regular job, but I was depressed. My family recommended that I go and see a shrink because something was wrong with me. I felt deeply sad. I still had dreams that my life was in danger. Then, one day, I had this strong urge to go to the library and find a book to read. I didn't know what book I was looking for, but I went to look for it. I scaled the isles until I came to a book that seemed to stand out on the shelf. This book was entitled "Maximize the Moment," written by Bishop T.D. Jakes. I will never forget that book because it was the tool Abba used to pivot my life. I don't know how I knew it was the book I was looking for, but I did.

I also now know that God led me to the answers I needed. I can only recall the chapter entitled, "Soul Aches". T.D Jakes began to describe accurately the aching deep down that I'd been experiencing. My heart pounded louder and louder the more I read in anticipation of the resolution. Finally, he said that the aches were "God's call to repentance, which simply means to turn around and go the other way" Oh, you don't know the joy that filled my heart. I wept in relief. That longing that we feel deep down on the inside that nothing can fulfill. We try so many things to fill it: sex, drugs, money, etc., but we still end up empty and sad. That's the place that only God can occupy and bring true peace that passes all understanding. I cried out to God that night, and I asked Him what I should do. His audible voice responded, "Get saved, or you will die!" Do you ever feel the urgency that something has to change, or you won't make it? The desperation that makes you cry out to God? That place is a sacred place. If you are there, can I encourage you? Your life is about to shift completely. There is an unspeakable joy that is going to bubble up in you. You see, without salvation, we die the second death, which is the lake of fire for eternity.

I admonish you as Abba admonished me that night. *Get saved or you will die!*

I apologize for saying it so frankly, but it is the truth. Stop running. Stop fighting God and come as you are. He understands your history and the battles you have faced because of it. He will not reject you. You will see that burden lifted and feel so light you will jump for joy! "And my spirit rejoices in God my Savior." Luke 1:47

I called a church about 4 blocks from my apartment, and a woman answered the phone. I was shocked! I believe it was a Thursday night. Although there were no services, she explained that her job was to be there to answer the phones. I cried out, explaining to her everything that had happened. She instructed me to come to the church. I arrived after 9 pm. She taught me about salvation and baptism. I received Jesus and was baptized that same night. She had called in one of the elders to baptize me. I left that church tangibly feeling different. I knew without a shadow of a doubt that I was made new. After going to this church for 2 services, the Lord instructed me to attend my childhood church. My godfather (the pastor) recognized me during my first service there and asked me to come up for prayer.

When I got to the altar, he revealed that he had been praying for me. The Spirit of the Lord began to inspire him with a word of knowledge. The pastor said, "Give God praise! Baby, if you knew how many times death came for you, but God commanded death to stand still!" At that moment, I remembered the dreams I was having where death was always chasing me, but could never catch me. I remembered the nightmares my mother was having of me being raped and strangled to death. And I recalled all the times, when I was in the strip club, where I felt someone watching me. I became overwhelmed with praise, and I lost all dignity and gave God the glory that was due Him. See, we owe Abba praise every day. There is so much Abba keeps us from. We don't know it all. I believe it would traumatize us if we did. So praise Him for keeping you. This is *your* moment!

"Because your love is better than life, my lips will glorify you. I will praise you as long as I live, and in your name, I will lift up my hands." Psalm 63:3-4

I believe you are reading my story because Abba wants you to know that the thing you've been struggling with all your life, "*An enemy has done it!*" The good news is that Abba knows how to uproot it. You needed to hear my story to see that you are not alone. Your struggle is not beyond help. Jesus declared in Matthew 15 that deliverance is the children's bread. This means that it's for God's own sons and daughters.

Renewing the Spirit of Your Mind

Ephesians 4:22-23 says, "Throw off your old sinful nature and your former way of life, which is corrupted by lust and deception. Instead, let the Spirit renew your thoughts and attitudes."

My journey of healing my sexuality and identity has not come without examining and challenging my belief system. Your belief system is the set of beliefs that you have about what is right and wrong and what is true and false. Some beliefs are lies at the subconscious level. Let me help you to understand. When going through an intense season of healing, severe anxiety disorder and depression manifested out of seemingly nowhere. All my spiritual leaders were saying it was a spirit of fear. One day, a woman of God came alongside me and asked me if I had asked God what the root of this problem was? My response was no. She encouraged me to ask God to reveal the root of the issue. In obedience, I went home and asked Abba why was I going through this. I confessed that I was in fear. God's audible voice said to me, "the root is not fear; it is unbelief!" I was flabbergasted. I have lived to believe Abba for supernatural manifestations since the day I gave Him my life. To hear Him tell me that I was living in unbelief was shocking. How could this be when I have had faith to see the supernatural? Boy, was I in for a revelation.

Later, I saw this woman and told her what God said to me, and she encouraged me to study scriptures on unbelief. She admonished me to spend the next week or two quiet before Abba because He was going to reveal to me where the root of this spirit was or at the moment the seed was planted. She educated me on the fact that more than likely, it would be a suppressed memory from some point in my life. This memory would be the moment this ungodly belief formed. Well, one week later, I experienced this moment. I was talking with a friend, and at the moment, I found myself back in my father's living room. Right there, He said he knew I was being emotionally & physically abused by his wife but needed me to help him keep the peace as he had 2 other daughters he was trying to raise. At that moment, I uttered only in my heart, "You coward! You mean you know she abuses me, and instead of protecting me, you want to keep the peace?" I was heartbroken. At that very moment, Abba audibly said to me, "Because your natural father didn't protect you, you don't believe that I will protect you."

I had totally suppressed this situation and forgot about it. Yet, it was affecting my relationship with Abba God at a subconscious level. It affected what I believed about Him, and I had no clue. It wasn't until I learned how to ask questions to get to the root of the issue that I was able to renew my mind in those areas with the Word of God and ascertain healing in my soul. I had to ask Abba to deal with my mind at the subconscious level by His Spirit as I consumed scriptures dealing with unbelief. Simultaneously, I would stand in the mirror, look myself in the eyes and command the spirit of unbelief to come out of my soul. This is casting demons out of yourself, and you can do it, too. Every time I was tempted to be fearful, I knew it was unbelief, and I did whatever it was, even if I was afraid (like flying in an airplane for the first time). I would quote scriptures like Psalm 91 to plant new seeds and build myself up in faith. I had to do things that forced me to confront my unbelief and trust God. Likewise, with any evil seed, you will have to be renewed in the spirit of your mind. Sexual sins are the same. There is usually a defining moment in your life where something happened, and you know you've never been the same since. Actions usually follow your true beliefs. It's time to be renewed in the spirit of your mind so that the root of sexual sin can be plucked out.

Identifying the Seed by Fruit Produced

"By their fruit, you will recognize them. Do people pick grapes from thornbushes, or figs from thistles? Likewise, every good tree bears good fruit, but a bad tree bears bad fruit. A good tree cannot bear bad fruit, and a bad tree cannot bear good fruit. Every tree that does not bear good fruit is cut down and thrown into the fire. Thus, by their fruit you will recognize them." Matthew 7:16-20

I want you to understand how to obtain healing and deliverance from these "evil seeds" that have taken root and grown to be trees producing harvest after harvest of darkness in your life. First, you have to learn to identify the fruit. Seeds produce after their own kind. Apple seeds give you a harvest of apples, pumpkin seeds give you a harvest of pumpkins. Likewise, in the spirit, fruit is produced. This fruit is evident in our speech, disposition, behaviors, actions, and motives. The Bible declares in James 3:11-12 NIV, "Can both fresh water and saltwater flow from the same spring? My brothers and sisters, can a fig tree bear olive or grapevine bear figs? Neither can a salt spring produce fresh water." It is imperative that we understand that deliverance and healing require getting down to the source or root of the matter. By inspecting fruit, you can identify the root, seed, or strongman that needs uprooting. This work can be painstaking, but it is a beautiful journey that will strengthen your faith and experience the supernatural love of God. You will experience supernatural transformation.

Even as I type this, I hear the Holy Spirit quoting a scripture that I hadn't thought of. The scripture is found in Hebrews 12:15-16 NLT, and it says, "Look after each other so that none of you fails to receive the grace of God. Watch out that no poisonous root of bitterness grows up to trouble you, corrupting many. See that no one is sexually immoral or is godless like Esau, who traded his birthright as the firstborn son for a single meal."

Let me be led entirely at this moment and explain what Abba is saying to you. I believe this one scripture sums up everything that I have been conveying up until this point while warning us what these evil seeds can produce if we don't deal with them.

This scripture warns of *falling away* from God due to an evil root. This evil root of bitterness will produce corrupt principles that lead to turning our backs on God. We then have Esau as an example in this scripture. Esau, as firstborn, had the privilege of a special blessing called the birthright. The birthright refers to the right of the firstborn to inherit his father's possessions and authority. Esau's sin was that he despised his birthright and sold it to enjoy sensual ease and pleasure. It was too late by the time Esau's conscience was convicted of his sin. Esau had more respect for his own appetite than his birthright.

In scripture, Abba refers to our appetite as our lusts. He says in Philippians 3:19 that there are those who are enemies of Christ's cross because their god is their bellies, and they only think about this life here on earth. Their end is destruction.

Beloved, this doesn't have to be so. I know we live in a time of a user-friendly Jesus, but the real Jesus warned us in his word by sobering reminders of neglecting so great of salvation. Like Esau, we are the firstborn (Romans 8:29), and our Heavenly Father has given us a birthright (Romans 8:17; Galatians 4:7). We have an inheritance. Don't sell your birthright for temporary pleasure. Take these principles and allow Abba to walk with you and assist you in dealing with these evil seeds that drive evil lusts and appetites. He loves you. There is nothing in your history or heart at this very moment that shocks Him. He's just waiting on you to surrender those areas, trusting that He will redeem them.

We can identify fleshly fruit from the fruit of the Spirit by studying Galatians 5:17-21 NIV. These verses tell us that the flesh desires that which is contrary to the Spirit. These two are in conflict or antagonistic to one another. It lists the acts/attributes of what is called, "the works of the flesh" in contrast to *the fruit of the Spirit* produced in one's life. Here's your homework: study each one. Use an online dictionary to have a thorough understanding of what each of these looks like. Then you will be able to identify them in your life. You will be equipped with the truth of God's word, which is enough to bring about a lasting change. I urge you to pray and ask Abba to supernaturally reveal each one to you and lay His holy ax to the root of each evil seed in your life. Those you find that you struggle with the most are where you want to stay and dig in deep. Enlist help from your local church, which brings me to my next point.

You Need a Tribe

Besides the fact that Abba tells us, "Do not fail to assemble together," we need to understand the benefits of fellowshipping together. James 5:16 tells us to confess our sins to one another and pray for each other so that we may be healed. The prayers of the righteous are powerful and effective. When we come together and pray for one another, it encourages us and produces healing. A biblical principle that I love to stand on declares, where two or more come together in God's name, He will be there in the midst, and whatever they ask, it will be done! How encouraging is this? You don't have to bear this alone. Abba has given us a family called the church, the actual wife of Christ. He takes full responsibility for it as its head. Don't underestimate the power of a spiritual family in your journey. Ask Abba to lead you to a good church, where He would have you join to become a productive, well-educated, well-equipped, and victorious member of the kingdom of Heaven. I also understand that some people may not feel ready to join a local church for many reasons. In that case, I would recommend online ministries. Otherwise, a good therapist can help you get to the root or the bottom of things that we find ourselves having a hard time overcoming.

Finally: The Blessing of the Pure

Blessed are the pure in heart, for they will see God. Matthew 5:8.

Pure represents many words in the Hebrew language. To be pure means to be free from defilement, to be cleansed with lye or alkali for soap, to have dross purged away, to be clean, sincere.

This scripture is one of my absolute favorites ever! Purity is powerful because it gets you a front-row seat with Abba. That excites me. I want to see Him up close and personal. Because of this, my purity is at the top of my list. Do I fall short of this ideal, at times? Yes! I never stop pressing to apprehend. I believe that this is why, despite my falling short of this ideal at times, I have had some powerful experiences with Abba. I remind Him that He promised to turn His hand upon me and purge away my dross and take away my sin. (Isaiah 1:25).

It is important to note that dross is the scum, rust, and waste matter of metals separated from them when heated to melting. Therefore, the real value of silver or gold only comes after the dross is removed. We are like precious metals in need of refining. This process happens in what the Bible calls the "furnace of affliction" Abba is the one who does this refining, personally. He states in Isaiah 48:10, "Behold, I have refined you, but not with silver; I have chosen you in the furnace of affliction."

This furnace is designed to be hot, which is not comfortable; but because we know that this fire is producing in us a far more precious eternal weight of glory, we submit or allow ourselves to melt under the mighty hand of God. The amazing thing is even though it doesn't feel good to your flesh, your spirit knows that it's good. You literally feel and see the hand of God at work in you. As it gets hot, things in you come to the surface. Don't be discouraged; this is what the fire is meant to do. All your impurities will surface!!! Understand that Abba is already aware of what's in you. What He is revealing to you, He is healing, but your submission is key. When this "dross" surfaces, turn to the Lord in prayer. Study the thing that surfaces out in scripture. Let Him know that you see it, thank Him for bringing it to the surface and removing it. This is the place where the worshipper is born. Worship takes you deeper in intimacy with Abba. A relationship is developing at an accelerated pace. Your righteousness increases, and you begin to see your desires switch. This is the place you began to see God. You are being purified. Hallelujah!

I weep in joy for your future. I am so excited about your purity. This journey doesn't come without challenges, but the benefits outweigh them all.

I pray that you find this place and excel from there to soar with Christ. I pray that you overcome with great power every planting of the devil! So, you would see the manifestation of all things working together for good, that you would prosper and be in health even as your soul prospers. May you walk in the place of purity and perpetually see God! In the name of our Lord and Savior, Jesus Christ, Amen.

I love you.

Crystal Townsend Bio

Crystal Townsend was born and raised in Detroit, Michigan. There she gave birth to a son in the year 2000 and married the love of her life, Jerome Townsend in 2006. The early part of Crystal's marriage was spent homeschooling her son and being a homemaker according to the direction of the Holy Spirit. Two years ago, Crystal and her husband relocated to Portland, OR. Crystal works in healthcare and is also a full-time student and licensed cosmetologist. Her ministry, Anointed for Beauty focuses on healing and deliverance for hurting women. Her passion is to see women of God whole and in love with Jesus.

Moving on by His Grace

THIS IS THAT

Debra Bernard

This year, I finally decided to take the challenge to write a chapter of my story. I am very excited about it as this is the perfect time in my life to invest my effort in launching a book. For several years, I have procrastinated because of fear. However, I'm excited (yet hesitant), but I must overcome this fear. So, I decided to move by faith and be willing to try to get it done. I have used my voice as my most vital way of communication for most of my life. But, today, using my writing skills will allow me to step into something new and different.

In the coaching workshops, we talked about some of the things that authors faced. And we were given guidance and shared information identifying obstacles that may hinder the writing process. I am so grateful for the additional coaching because it was necessary for my patience and that extra boost of confidence needed. The second challenge for me is my lack of skills in using technology. There are no excuses allowed in my mind. I can do all things through Christ that strengthens me (Phil 4:13)

I have experienced many times when the Lord was leading me to another level, answering a question I have asked. It can be challenging if I try to figure it out. I have to trust and believe in what I know about faith in God, take the step, apply the action, and do the work. I will definitely pay attention to the upcoming days to see how God will manifest this assignment. I asked God for more closeness. In this season, I want to be and do what he has proposed for me to do. The hindrances delaying the progress of production must go, in Jesus' name.

Every day I have set time for writing, and the morning after prayer seems to be a "God" time. I started to write on a subject; I was everywhere. I became disturbed and frustrated. I prayed and meditated on a couple of scriptures (Psalm 34:1b), "But they that seek the Lord shall not want for any good thing," and 2 Corinthians 2:14a, "Now thanks be unto God which always causes us to triumph in Christ." It was the beginning of "that." I realized "this" strategy in faith would be the key to overcoming fear and completing the assignment.

The title of my story immediately came into my mind "This Is That." I am convinced by the book's title, *Moving on by His Grace*, that I will learn to increase with success in the days to come. I am taking on a more significant attitude with confidence. As I took my position to write, something extraordinary began to happen. My body began to feel uncomfortable. I experienced something physically happening. My hands became clammy; my heartbeat was racing; I was anxiously stressing within my emotions. It was so crazy. I asked myself, what is this? I heard in my spirit loudly, "This is that." At that moment, I felt paralyzed, unable to move. I decided to get up from the table to drink some tea and take a break. There were times in the past when participating in unfamiliar new tasks, would cause my anxiety to rise. I learned fear would manifest itself in different ways. I also became more determined to wait a moment and just be still. I returned to my table. I began to type. I thought about the book's title and how my story would be relative. When I was younger, an incident from my past came to mind, drawing me towards revisiting "that" memory. I knew this was the time I needed to address it.

My life growing up was pretty sheltered. Hanging out in the streets was not an option for me. My parents were middle-class educators with high expectations for my sister and me. We were continuously engaged in a variety of activities, culturally and recreationally. I loved to travel too, and visiting relatives on the road trips was a summer treat. I enjoyed having a fun time with my sisters and parents. It wasn't until middle school that I went through my first and most traumatic experience. After that, I remembered my whole perspective of life began to change. In the late 60's and early 70's, racial tensions within the world started to rise. In Detroit, violence with rioting, looting, beatings, stealing, and police brutality infiltrated our neighborhood. I was exposed to fear in a way that devastated me, mentally and emotionally. When the riots ceased, I was reluctant to freely move around the neighborhood, for some time.

I was a part of the integration in the school system. I will never forget the day when my mother told me I would not be able to attend the local middle school. I would have to be bussed to the middle school out of my community and district. This was my first time dealing with an experience I was totally naive about. I had never been exposed to racism.

My parents taught me to respect everyone and would try to prepare me for future encounters in my life by sharing their personal stories, educating me with selective books, and exposing me to stage plays. I'm grateful. However, reading a book to bring awareness and living through the experience are not the same. Racism in my community wasn't apparent. We had white neighbors on both sides of our house. We never had any outbursts or discord with one another. I would sometimes go to one of our neighbors' houses after school if my parents were going to be late coming from work. They were exceptionally friendly people and were good to all of us. On our block, the children played with one another. We could not cross the street or leave the block. Some adults would be sitting on the porch, while others would wash cars in the driveway or mow their lawns, always looking out for one another. The beauty and barbershops were two houses down from our home on the corner. On Saturdays, we would sit on the porch and watch people with new hairstyles and fresh haircuts parade out of the shops, styling while profiling. Sometimes they would throw a couple of dollars our way to spend at the corner store adjacent to the shops. Our school was about six blocks from the house. All of the children were within walking distance and felt safe. I shared all of this information to paint a picture of how secure and safe I felt in my life.

From my perspective and environment, thinking about being bussed was the extreme opposite of what I experienced while growing up. First of all, standing, waiting, and catching the bus was time-consuming as I had to board three. The entire trip one way took two hours. This feeling of inward fear was still a part of my memory. The Holy Spirit wanted me to recognize and identify this feeling from that experience. God is revealing something to me through this writing. The Holy Spirit is teaching me to identify and release fear as I learn and apply His word.

When I face these profound and subtle experiences of victimization or abuse, this fear attack presents itself through writing this story. I can clearly see how many adverse situations can significantly impact the body physically, mentally, spiritually, or emotionally. I began to feel overwhelmed; tears filled my eyes. I got up from the table, grabbed my coat, and decided to go for a walk. The memory caused me to reflect on the previous middle-school incident and the times of having to exchange buses three times. There were twelve black students in the group catching the bus. The trauma and terror of that fear unveiled so many different emotions. The result of that fear lying dormant with no resolve or closure took root in my soul. I was devastated and so angry. I couldn't understand the depth of what I was experiencing within myself until it all unfolded. The following incident after getting off the bus terrified all of us. We had to walk a mile after getting off the bus to the school. White people on every porch were yelling, "Niggas go home!" They had dogs on leashes ready to attack us, and shouting profanity while telling us we didn't deserve to walk down their street. There was no protection. We ran together so tightly, as fast as we could. I don't know how, but we did. We told the administration upon arrival. We also called our parents. This process took about three weeks before police escorts were made available for our safety. We all carpooled as our parents met with the school officials and demanded a resolution.

This memory is one I had to confront and heal the emotions attached to this experience. My parents agreed to in-school counseling sessions with the school counselor for the duration of the time until the fear subsided. The vast number of mental feelings and emotions included anger, rage, and revenge. The counseling helped me overcome this by sharing these experiences from my perspective. I also was given information and ways to confront the trauma and be healed. I realize keeping traumatic incidents hidden without asking for help is not the best way to handle loving one's true self.

I try to work on myself in my relationship with God every day. Fear is real. The trauma attached to fear is more complicated than just casting out demons in deliverance. God's love is the only cure to fix who and what we are today. I have discovered it is about the totality of His love. It is how we develop connection to the way God originally created us to be in the expressed image of who He is. It is a heart thing. In my next book, I believe I will share the process of my life experiences through my growth and maturity in the faith. The truth is that God created everything in love because He is love. Everyone reading this story is searching for God's love. I believe the kingdom of God by His Grace has drawn you to this book. It is your time and season. The depth of this experience proved *this is that*, and life continues on.

Women usually endure and harness emotional energy connected to pain. And that feeling of lacking personal fulfillment or a sense of being loved. However, many of us attempt to deal with our desire to be loved and feel whole and complete. It is sometimes interrupted by thoughts of disappointment, low self-esteem, self-worth, or lack of self-value. This void can affect the heart, leaving us with negative thinking and creating a toxic environment in our minds. Negative emotions can include depression, loneliness, codependency, and self-sabotage, leading to self-destructive decisions. This energy is dangerous. This particular experience laid dormant for 54 years inside me, which may have contributed to my cancer diagnosis in 2017. Today, I am completely healed with faith in God, His Word, and His Grace. I truly Thank God for the Holy Spirit for revealing this incident. I let it all go! I asked God to cast down every thought and experience connected to fear as far as the east is to the west, never to be remembered anymore. (Psalm 103:12).

Today, I am now writing my chapter with a sense of confidence. God confirmed for me through this writing that He was doing a new thing in my life. I am reminded of a scripture, "Therefore if any man be in Christ, He is a new creature. Old things are passed away; behold, all things become new. (2 Cor. 5:17). I feel very inspired.

I had an invitation today to have breakfast with a couple of friends at my favorite breakfast spot. We were sitting in the booth talking, laughing, and having a ball. One of my friends brought up the subject of family. While expressing her opinion, the volume of her voice began to respond to frustration. I immediately heard the words, "This is that" in my mind. When she was talking about a particular person in her family, I realized there was some unresolved disturbance between the two of them.

I knew that she needed this moment to share what she was feeling. My friend needed to be free. Each one of us contributed to consoling and quieting her spirit.

God is in us with His guidance through the Holy Spirit. Everyone at the table shared a personal experience relative to family dysfunction. The conversation created a safe, trusting environment. I could identify a variety of emotional hurt, pain, anger, and holding back of unresolved truths lying dormant within the group. I just witnessed another example of fear operating in others. It was a moment relative to my writing assignment. The spirit of love was in our gathering. The sharing, caring, building trust, getting free, and releasing internal toxicity was evident in God answering my prayer. I identified with the word, "There is no fear in love, but perfect love casts out all fear because fear has to do with punishment. The one who fears is not made perfect in love". (1 John 4:18)

The title, *Moving on by His Grace* is eye-opening for me. I am reflecting on the importance of taking responsibility and accountability for my purpose in life. Who am I, and why am I here? These are questions that began at the age of thirty, and today at age sixty-six, I am still on the journey, but this time void of fear and replacing it with faith. "Trust in the Lord with all your heart and lean not to your own understanding; in all your ways acknowledge him; He shall direct your pathway." (Psalm 119:11). I thank God for encouraging me to have the faith and the courage to continue writing my story. To God be the glory.

Every living human being on this earth is here for a reason. The identifying purpose is learned by identifying your true self. In life, regardless of the experiences, every decision made has consequences based on knowledge or ignorance. Surround yourself with people representing what you aspire to be. It is important to have resources outside of yourself that will provide wisdom with insight and information to assist with making decisions when you don't have answers. There are resources and methods to seek information, such as self-help books, videos on you-tube, counselors, and life coaches. However, it is up to the individual to seek out what personal belief system works for them.

This story is dedicated to women searching for truth and direction in life. The truth begins with deciding to change the place you are in presently, be honest with yourself, and seek outside help. God, as my Source along with The Holy Bible as the resource manual answered every problem I encountered in life. God and His Word will provide trust, loyalty, commitment, protection, and fulfillment.

Fear is associated with a lack of understanding and the unknown. It creates darkness. Ignorance means lack of knowledge. The feeling of being stuck, repeating the same mistakes, trapped, just wanting to get free from feeling mentally imprisoned creates bondage. There are times when the resolve of this torment in life suggests being hard on ourselves, desperate to escape the guilt without hope or any support to be encouraged.

I recall many times in my early years, I would pray, go to church, and read my Bible. At that time, I also needed help understanding my own personal difficulties. I needed to be able to talk truthfully about my private hidden thoughts. Talking with a spiritual therapist/counselor helps with conflicts. I learned how to love self and practically apply what was read, instead of turning to the wrong places and people for answers.

It is essential to have a mature individual helping you that is non-judgmental. Also, it is equally important to identify triggers and eliminate those related to toxic behavior. I decided after my life had improved tremendously from self-destruction. It went from spinning out of control to having faith. I received support, learned how to trust God by reading the word, and being guided to the Light. This was the type of knowledge that I needed to change. I remember asking God to save me. Finally, I found a church where I could understand the teaching. I matured, served, and became strong and courageous. When my life turned around, I found out consciously; that the decisions I succumbed to for change were necessary and were all for my good.

Moving on By His Grace is when L.I.F.E (Love is forever evolving) is given to each human being for a purpose. No matter when and what you go through, love is the foundation within you, and there is only one of you. Therefore, learn as much about yourself as possible before engaging in outside relationships with others.

Debra Bernard Bio

Debra Bernard is my name. At 66 years old, I have had many experiences and much to learn. I am a mother of five children and a grandmother of 10 grandchildren. Some of the various roles I have taken up include a student at Hampton Institute of Virginia and University of Phoenix, where I obtained my Masters in Business and Bachelors of Science in Education. I have served as an administrator in the United States Air Force, a certified Life Coach practitioner, an educator of 30 years, a minister of the gospel of reconciliation and founder of P.R.A.I.S.E (Positive Reinforcement Assures Individual Self Esteem). What inspired me to write this piece was my experiences with fear. It was faith in God that helped me to love and live my life because God is love and love is forever evolving (L.I.F.E).

Moving on by His Grace

MOVING FORWARD BY FAITH

Deborah Glass

In my senior year, I was hired by a company in Corporate America under an apprenticeship while at Central High School. My mother was proud of the opportunity I was given and looked at it as if I had made it to the WNBA. But unfortunately, in my experience, as I relate to society today, I can see that much has not changed for us as people of color. We must prove that even though we may be as qualified and often overqualified, we are sometimes still met with much opposition.

As the only black supervisor and female in my department, I was often attacked by a predominantly all-white male establishment in our supervisor's meetings. When I watched on TV the proceeding of our first black woman, Ketanji Brown Jackson, to serve as a judge on the Supreme Court, I had flashbacks. It was the same demeanor and tone used in our meetings towards me. I felt so bad for her. I know what that feels like. When you are attached to that type of setting, they want you to react angrily. I remember my white supervisor calling me into a management meeting, asking me to share with them how I was able to come up with so many good ideas in the department. I explained to them how important it is to think outside the box. I also said, there are times you may run into some opposition because people don't like change.

My supervisor called me out of the meeting to tell me I was offensive because I used the word opposition. They would go out of their way to try and humiliate me. They know if they can get you to lose it, then they will say you aren't qualified for the job. They often gave my white co-workers credit for my ideas and promoted them instead of me.

Being a female in the workplace has had its challenges. Often white males are given promotions and raises just because they are white. I will never forget when I discovered there was a system in place to promote white males. It just so happens that I was going through the employees' files that I supervised. I had females and two white males that reported directly to me; the females didn't have much in their files. I discovered a letter explaining why they had not been promoted in the two white males' files. The letter was dated and documented when my supervisor had spoken to them. And it was as if he had to report this information to someone. Also, he noted that he tried to promote them, but they refused to take the jobs because they liked what they were doing. The letter stated that they had turned down the promotions on more than one occasion. But the part that got my attention was my supervisor's comments. He said that he would keep working on trying to get them to change their mind! No females, black or white, had a letter in their files explaining why they had not been promoted.

Women have never been given the same opportunities as men. We are still trying to break that glass ceiling no matter what we do. In my case, it seems I was fighting a losing battle. Being a woman and being black, I was a double minority. White men and white women have received promotions and raises just because of the color of their skin. Also, white women are considered a minority which pushed us back even further. And it is not that we aren't as smart or as intelligent. I find we were more than qualified in many cases, just like our new Supreme Court Judge Ketanji Brown Jackson.

Sometimes, we are so devalued that we don't think we deserve what is given to them. While on the other hand, I found the opposite of their thinking is entitlement. It's not what they say to you that should matter; however, it's what you say to yourself. No one can make you feel inferior without your permission. Stop co-signing what others say about you and start believing what GOD said about you in (Psalms 139: 13-14)) that you are fearfully and wonderfully made. Remember that GOD calls us who we are *before* we become it, and man calls us who we are *after* we become it. After many years of disappointment, I decided to work unto God and not unto Man.

While still working in corporate America, I was introduced to the Amway company by a couple named Al and Fran Hamilton. They were Black Diamonds making over two hundred thousand a year in the Amway business. That's not including the free trips and bonuses they received regularly. They both had quit their corporate American jobs in their twenties and worked their Amway business together. They came to my home to show me a business opportunity. They asked me, "Where do you want to be 30 years from now?". No one had ever asked me that question. I was still in my twenties. My response was that "I want to be retired from corporate America, living in a high-rise downtown apartment overlooking the Detroit River." They had a board and easel set up in my living room, and they wrote FREEDOM on the board. They said Deborah, you want your freedom, and we will show you how to get it. That night I became an (IBO) Independent Business Owner. They introduced my husband and I to the Bill Britt system. When he was introduced to the Amway business, Bill Britt was a city manager. He became a multi-millionaire in the Amway business. He helped many others like Al and Fran to be wealthy by using his system and had one of the largest organizations in the Amway Corporation. He believed in the Bible and taught us the word of God from scriptures that supported us having wealth (Deuteronomy 8:18).

The Bill Britt system also happens to be the same system that taught Steve Harvey biblical success principles about wealth when he was in the Amway business. Steve often teaches, motivates, and encourages others using these success principles. Bill Britt taught us straight out of the Bible to *put God first!*

We learned how to speak to the mountains in our lives according to Mark 11:23. We understood that our words were seeds, and we get what we speak. If you want to change your circumstance, it starts with changing what you say. If you say you are broke, then chances are you're broke. If you say you can't, then you can't, but the good news is if you say you can, you can. He taught us the scripture (Proverbs 18:21) power of life and death is in the tongue.

We were taught to have a big dream, so big that it would take God to make it happen. You must have a big dream that motivates you to get up early and keeps you up late. I learned that if your dream is big enough, the facts don't count. Find a way to get it done. We were taught to do vision boards and write our dreams down. We were instructed to put them on a vision board (Habakkuk 2:2) to visualize what you want. If your dream is to have a big house, find a picture of the home you want and put it on the board. If it is a car, put a picture of the vehicle you want on the board. If you need money to pay for your kids' college, put pictures of them on your board. If you're going to get out of debt, write it down on the board.

My vision board had the word freedom on it. Then I added a picture of a lady relaxing as if she didn't have a care in the world. That picture was the first thing I saw in the morning and the last thing I saw before bed. That board motivated me. I got what was on my board and on every vision board I ever created after that. So just start dreaming again and believing that you can have it.

We learned the power of unity and working together (Psalm 133). We built powerful teams together and traveled many places as we built our businesses. We developed great friendships, many of them we still have to this day. *Teamwork makes the dream work*!

Unlike my job in corporate America, you must step on each other to get to the top. Amway became my escape from the bondage of corporate America. Even though we never made it to the Diamond level in the Amway business, we made a lot of money and friends. I learned more about the Bible and how to use the word of God in my everyday life than I have learned anywhere else. Amway became my way of escape from politics, racism, injustice, sexism, and inequality.

I was able to complete 30 years in corporate America. I have a full retirement. Oh, by the way, I live downtown in a high-rise apartment overlooking the Detroit River.

After I retired from the corporate world, I was blessed to start my own hair business company called Black Pride Beauty LLC. I was visiting my daughter-in-love, and she was wearing hair extensions, but I noticed her hair kept getting thinner. She had long thick beautiful hair, and I didn't understand why she was damaging her hair and scalp. I asked her how she was adding the hair, and she explained that she was using sew-in and glue in. I decided to go buy some hair weave and look for some combs to add to the hair weave. I sewed the combs on the hair weave and asked her to try using that method to add to her hair extensions. She loved wearing it, but her head was sore at the end of the day. I had to figure out how to fix that problem, but I knew I was on to something. After I had solved that problem, I filed for a design and utility patent to protect my idea. If you have an idea and can't afford a patent, do a provisional patent while you do your research.

I am asked often how did I come up with that idea? I asked God to give me something that I could do that would help black people to circulate dollars back in our community. This is what He gave me!

If you want to know what God has for you to do, you must ask Him. That's what I did. It is a faith journey. I had to ask God how to get through every hurdle, and there were many. So I developed a book that I go to for all my help and answers. It doesn't replace the Bible, but is a tool that will help you create a stronger relationship with Him. The name of it is "Ask God, My Journal of Prayer Requests" by Deborah Glass. I have several of these books that I use filled with prayer requests and God's answers (Mark 11:24). You can order it on Amazon or go to my website (see below), and you will get the black and red ink pen with your book. Every time I ran into a roadblock, I would go to my journal and write my prayer request in black ink. Then, I would listen for GOD to give my next set of instructions. Then I would write the answer in red ink. Just like in the Bible, when Jesus spoke, it was written in red. This is how I was able to stay encouraged when it seemed like nothing was going right. I had many days I wanted to throw in the towel and give up, but my dream was so big that I had to fight for it. I applied everything I was taught in the Amway business to my business. The biblical success principles work on anything you apply them to.

I believe my product will circulate dollars back into our community. I am working with salon owners and other business partners to put a system in place to make that happen. There are numerous hair products on the market, but nothing can do what this product can and will do for our community. The product will hit the market this year. *To God Be the Glory!* I did it! Thank you, Jesus!

For more information, go to my website www.deborahglassenterprises.com

Deborah Glass Bio

Entrepreneur, Author, Educator, Patent Consultant, Inventor, Speaker, and Faith Coach.

As a believer and consistently on a journey for growth and discovery, **Deborah Glass** focused on her passion for entrepreneurship. After retirement in 2002, is became a burning desire for Deborah to discover what was going to be next in her life.

A relative was experiencing hair loss and not getting good results from hairstylists. Deborah was able to design and patent an innovative Comb-N-Weave hair piece, No Sew No Glue and No Clip for all ethnic groups of women. Her design would prevent further damage to the hair and scalp of many women. www.blackpridebeauty.com.

Deborah developed a journal called ASK GOD that teach you how to go to GOD with your prayer request and write it down in black ink but when GOD answers your prayer, you record it in red ink. It doesn't replace the Bible. It is a tool that will help you build a closer relationship with GOD. The book is sold on Amazon but if you go to the website and order you will get the red and black ink pens with your book. www.deborahglassenterprises.com

…ye have not, because ye ask not. – James 4:2 (KJV).

TRANSFORMED BY GRACE

Elder Geneva James

Today, I am a woman who has overcome fear. The enemy had me bound all of my life by fear. God delivered me from the spirit of fear in 2019 when he gave me a word in I John 4:18, "There is no fear in love, but perfect love casteth out fear: because fear hath torment. He that feareth is not made perfect in love."

When I read 2 Timothy 1:7, "For God hath not given us the spirit of fear, but of power, love, and a sound mind." This stuck with me my whole life. When you have a house payment (rent), it is due on the 1st of the month; what happens if it is not paid by the 5th of the month? The grace period runs out, and you accumulate a late fee and receive an eviction notice. The eviction notice informs that you have allotted days to vacate the property. My grace period was up!

In the dictionary, grace is defined as courteous goodwill, but according to Ephesians 2:8-9, it's God's kindness and gracious generosity. This message is written to those who are hiding their pain with alcohol. God is releasing you now as you read this chapter. Praise and thank God for your deliverance, just as he delivered me from the bondage of alcohol. He can do it for you! No more alcohol! Depend on God and trust him! Keep believing as he leads you to your destiny. Amen! After that, I began to read and rely on scriptures. I thought the scriptures were only speaking to me, and when I went to work, I would show some of the ladies what the prophets in the Bible revealed to me. Although I didn't really believe that the Bible was for me, the desire to read it stayed with me.

One day, a close friend of mine, Janice Knight, (now deceased) told me about Pastor Corletta Harris, who opened a Bible College. She thought we should attend. I agreed and called the college to get more details. The best news was that the classes started the same day I called. This college introduced me to Holy Ghost Full Gospel Church. After visiting the church every week, I joined and then the church moved to 1745 East Grand Blvd. Pastor Harris changed the school's name to Ministers in Training.

I felt like giving up some days, but I praise God that I didn't. I remembered 2 Chronicles 15:7 "Be ye strong therefore, and let not your hands be weak: for your work shall be rewarded."

My Personal Obstacles

I didn't think that I would make it. I would tell myself you are too old, too busy, and have a southern accent. Why did you get into this class? You don't belong here! You're not a school teacher, doctor, or an educated person; but I kept coming and pushing through. I remembered a sermon Pastor C preached at that time, and the message was "Determination Defeats the Enemy." I had many things that happened in my life to discourage me, and all I knew was that I had to keep pushing. I refused to "look back" like

Lot's wife in Genesis 19:26. "But his wife looked back from behind him, and she became a pillar of salt."

The Bible indicates that those who "look back" dwell in the past and can be destroyed. Fear, bitterness, and un-forgiveness persist when you live in the past. When a person continually looks back to the past, they are poised to backslide. They're making their past their future. I continue to move forward Philippians 3:14 "I press toward the mark for the prize of the high calling of God in Christ Jesus." No matter what has happened in my life, I have to keep moving. I have felt like giving up, but I have to keep moving.

My Family

I was the only child for five years and very spoiled. My parents, grandmother, and two aunts who didn't have their own children gave me everything I asked for. When my mother started to have other children, I spent more time at my grandmother's house and have many great memories. My parents would drink whiskey on the weekends, and it started to extend to them drinking throughout the week. I became afraid of them hurting each other. When I would hear a siren outside, I thought something had happened to one of them. My grandmother lived three doors down from my parents. I would spend time down in the country with my great grandmother and my uncles and their families in the summer. It was a large farming community, and my great-grandmother owned the land. My great-grandfather died when I was three or four years old. In the evenings, after they were finished working in the fields, everybody would sit on the porch, and my aunts and uncles would tell stories about ghosts called "haints." They didn't know that they were instilling a spirit of fear in me. I don't know how my other cousins felt, but I was terrified. I would cover my head up at night because I thought I would see a ghost. I was full of anxiety with low self-esteem. The list included fear of dead people, elevators, and closed spaces. Praise be to God because he delivered me from the spirit of fear in 2019. Paul tells Timothy in 2 Timothy 1:7 that "God has not given us a spirit of fear; but of power, love, and a sound mind."

Spirit of Fear

Fear caused me to withdraw into my own little world. I was what people would call a coward or timid. I didn't know that God didn't want me to be like that, or that I didn't have to be. Fear stems from ignorance of the word of God and from having a wrong mindset. Romans 12:2 tell us, "And be not conformed to this world: but be ye transformed by the renewing of your mind that ye may prove what that good, and acceptable, and perfect, will of God."

My father acted more like a brother to me than a father, maybe because he grew up without a father and didn't know how to be a father. I believed this made me want to feel loved by a man. I would listen to love songs on the radio by the Platters called, "Smoke Gets in Your Eyes" and "It's All in the Game" by Tommie Edwards. I met my husband-to-be when I was fifteen years old, and the first time we had sex, I became pregnant. When my mom found out I was pregnant, she was upset. I was already six months along and hid it. Finally, both of our moms sat down and talked, and he said he would marry me, but instead he left town and went to Indiana to live with his brothers. He returned after I had a baby boy, and I named him Stanley. We got married when my baby boy was seven months, and I was pleased to be married and have my own family.

Same Old Pattern

Things were good during the week, but on the weekends, my parents' pattern became my own. He would drink whisky on the weekends and act crazy and sometimes even fight. That old spirit of fear that had me bound, crept back in, and I was so afraid. I remember running and hiding when he would act up, which would happen most weekends. I told myself I would never drink alcohol, but when we went to my sister-in-law's house, they would drink alcohol and listen to music. This was our entertainment. This became our way of life on the weekends because everyone had a job and worked during the week. The weekend became relaxation time. Everyone would say, "Come on, just have one drink. It won't hurt you!" I began taking sips of whiskey, which made me sick. I started out with a beer which didn't make me sick, and I kept drinking. That's how my habit began; even though I said I would never drink because of what my parents went through with drinking alcohol.

A few years later, we moved to Detroit, and my husband picked up employment at Chrysler. Everything went well with the job, and we moved in with his brother and family. My sister-in-law kept beer in the house. She didn't work, so drinking beer was what she did. She would always insist that I have a beer with her. I would say ok even though I didn't want to. I had a lack of self-control, or was this fear *again*? I felt like I needed to please her, so I began to drink beer frequently like she did. My husband would go out every weekend with "the guys" (his friends), and my sister-in-law and I would drink and listen to music. Drinking is how I coped with him going out and feeling neglected by him.

After moving out of my in-law's home, my husband continued to go out every weekend, leaving me at home alone with the children. I didn't mind being at home with the kids because they were my life. Unfortunately, my drinking increased. I wanted to escape the problems and pain. Adding insult to injury, my immediate family was far away, down south. I missed my parents and siblings. When my youngest turned two years old, I started to work at an envelope manufacturing company. After work, we would go out, and those who drank would get beer or whiskey. By this time, I started to drink whiskey and pick it up a small bottle after work from the local neighborhood store. Later, I began to drink vodka and would purchase a half pint and drink it until I was drunk and would go to bed. Usually, I would only drink on the weekends, but it became an everyday habit for years.

One day, I woke up at 10 a.m. at my sister-in-law's house. I had missed work. My husband took the children home and left me there overnight. The drinking continued for years and became my comfort.

I knew my husband was out with other women, and soon as I found out about one, he had moved on to the next! I soon found out he had another child, which hurt me, so badly. I asked him, "How could you do that?" He didn't give me an excuse. I told him that I hoped the child died. The baby girl did die, and I felt terrible for saying it. I began drinking even more because of the guilt for saying what I said about the baby and it actually happening.

After having one of my baby girls, one of my close girlfriends visited to see the new baby. I noticed my husband was acting strangely. Usually, he would cook and clean after I had a baby. This time around, after our fifth child, it wasn't the same; not to mention it was a Friday evening. So I knew he was going out. Shortly after, he confirmed he was going out. All of a sudden, my so-called "girlfriend" said, "I thought I had a date for tonight." I asked myself why would she say that in front of my husband? Her husband was his friend. I thought she shouldn't have said that in front of my husband. He left and said I'm going out for a while, and I'll be back. He left and my friend left shortly after. But guess what happened? My girlfriend and my husband went to a motel that night. Her husband trailed and caught them. My husband ran off so fast, he left the car. When he came into the house, I didn't hear him drive up. As he entered the house, I asked him where his car was. He said it ran out of gas, and he had walked home. He said he would get the car in the morning. Throughout the years, he would have different girlfriends, and I would drink more (destroying myself) when I found out.

One of his girlfriends, the one he eventually left me for, would leave her belongings like shoes or floral Kleenex in the car for me to find. I would ask him about it, and he would lie and say he took Jimmy and his girlfriend home from a gambling party. Being out gambling was always his excuse. Sometimes, he would stay out

Friday and Saturday nights and lose all his money. During this time, my furnace went out. He didn't attempt to get it fixed because he was so busy running the streets. Shortly after, the gas was turned off, and he brought home Kerosene heaters to keep the kids and me warm. To refill the 5-gallon Kerosene heaters, we had to take them to the gas station. He didn't care because he drove an eighteen-wheeler tractor-trailer and was gone out of town a lot. For six years, we lived this way.

Because he didn't pay the electric bill I also had the electricity turned back on, but we still used the Kerosene heaters for the heat source. I was so lost that my oldest daughter and oldest son joined the Armed Forces and weren't home when we didn't have heat. Then, I found a checkbook in my husband's coat pocket, and it had his and his girlfriend's names on it, and that's when things started to change. I wasn't looking for anything but ran across it while using his jacket to run to the store. When he returned home, I asked him about the checkbook, and he said, "If you don't like what I'm doing, you can get your ass out!"

I, then, started to seek God and ask for guidance, and God blessed me! So I began to pray, and the Holy Spirit came over me, and that's the day I believe I gained my freedom from him. Shortly after, he left me for another woman and would repeatedly betray me! How could he leave me for another woman? Since I was a very young girl, I've been with him and bore six children with him. When something like this happens, you look at yourself and say, "What's wrong with me?" This happened after I stopped drinking, and I don't think I would still be alive if I had continued to drink. I would have drunk myself to death.

Before I stopped drinking, I believe I was near death. It got to the point that I was so sick that I couldn't take another drink. Usually, I would take another drink and feel better when I had a hangover. There was a time I was so sick that I couldn't vomit or anything. I was so ill!

I was depressed because he stayed in the streets, and my primary care doctors prescribed depression pills to help me cope. The medication made me so sleepy that I couldn't get out of bed. I slept one day until two o'clock in the afternoon, and I knew then I had to do something to help myself.

This was a turning point for me, and I knew where I was headed if I didn't stop drinking. I was headed for the cemetery because of self-destruction according to Psalms 35:8 "Let destruction come upon him at unawares; and let his net that he hath hid catch himself: into that very destruction let him fall."

Praise be to God for all he has done for me. I used to get drunk after work and return to work with a hangover from the night before. My supervisor told me that I was a "drunk sot" one day. I didn't know what it meant at the time, but I knew it was something terrible. God used her to help me wake up. Sometimes when I would go on my drunken spree, I wouldn't go to work. I was depressed because of my husband. I stayed out a whole week, and my supervisor called me and asked if I still wanted my job. I told her, yes! She told me to report to work tomorrow on time, and I could keep my job, which was God's mercifulness and grace.

One_day the Holy Spirit gave me this scripture, 1 Corinthians 10:12-13. I internalized this scripture, read, and repeated it repeatedly to myself until it became a part of me. Every time I was tempted, the Holy Spirit reminded me of this scripture and brought it back to me. I stood on this word ever since, about forty-two years ago.

Transformed by His grace

Romans 12:2 "And be not conformed to this world: but be ye transformed by the renewing of your mind, that ye may prove what is that good, and acceptable, and perfect, will of God." There is a way out for those struggling with fear and who don't know the way to freedom. God's grace kept me until I came to my senses and recognized that He was with me.

Pivot Point

After work one day, I watched the 700 Club, and Pat Robertson talked to a woman who was telling her story about being delivered from alcoholism. As she described her challenges, I could relate because I faced the same challenges. A light came on in my head, and I realized, *I am an alcoholic!* I called the 700 Club, and a woman answered and prayed with me, and this started me on my journey of deliverance. Shortly after, I made an appointment with my Internal Medicine Doctor, and he referred me to a support group for alcoholics. He also gave me a prescription for Antabuse, which would make me sick if I drank alcohol while taking medicine. I decided not to take it because I had faith that God had delivered me from being an alcoholic. Hebrews 11:3 "Through faith, we understand that the worlds were framed by the word of God so that things which are seen were not made of things which do appear." I started to attend Vernon Chapel AME Church under the leadership of Pastor Brockington, which started my transformation.

Transformation is a process and a metamorphosis, meaning that you are changing from the person you are now into a completely different person by the power of the Holy Spirit. My freedom from the bondage of alcohol began when I acknowledged that I was an alcoholic. My mind had to be renewed. If it had not been for God's grace, I would still be serving alcohol, self, and Satan. When I read Romans 12:2, "Do not be conformed any longer to the pattern of this world, but e transformed." He made a total change in my nature and enabled me to be free daily.

My Calling

He told me to go back to the alcoholic and tell them what I did to save your soul. You will be delivered from the bondage of alcohol and drugs. I am telling you this so that you can reclaim your identity. I lost my identity, but God brought me through so that I could tell that you can be free. Walk-in your freedom. Chains have been broken. I hope you understand that by reading my story and seeing what God did for me, He can do the same for you! You can be transformed by his grace.

I am writing this to help other women know that they don't have to deal with situations of neglect, abuse, and betrayal. Especially to my young mothers raising their children, who have traditionally been raised to think they have to accept this kind of abuse. Traditional southern women teach their daughters that a piece of a man is better than no man at all! It's just not true.

After I started attending Vernon Chapel A.M.E. Church. I would listen and study and meditate on the word of God. Meditating on the word of God will help you when temptations come; you have something to help you resist him, and he will flee.

I want to encourage the women whose husband has left them for another woman to be strong. Don't use alcohol, face your fears. Seek God even though you may be weary and think God may not be there. He will come through and He will help you. These are some things that may help you:

1. When I turned my life around, I did not miss a Sunday at church. It's something about being in God's presence and getting the Word of God that makes a difference.

2. I would talk to an older lady who had been delivered from alcoholism a year before, and she was able to help me and identify with me if she saw me struggling. Find someone that you can talk to and be transparent with.

3. I read the Bible and books on alcoholism. I was determined to stay free!! I talked to my Pastor and told him what God had done for me. He told me to speak with him once a week, letting him know how I was doing. He said he would keep me in his prayers,

4. If you need a support group such as AAA or a counselor, seek one out until you are strong enough to do it alone.

5. Find a Bible-believing church and tell the Pastor what you are trying to overcome. They will guide you.

6. The devil will never stop trying to discourage, tempt or bring fear. God did not give us a spirit of fear but power, love, and a sound mind. 2 Timothy 1:7.

7. Get with like-minded people with whom you can share, talk, and be transparent. Corinthians 1:10 "Now I beseech you, brethren, by the name of our Lord, Jesus Christ, that ye all speak the same thing, and that there be no divisions among you; but that ye be perfectly joined together in the same mind and the same judgment."

God has a plan and a purpose for your life. You can do this!

Testimony

The devil told me that I was too old; everything was over. I retired five years ago. My friend called me asking if I knew someone who needed a job. Her company needed a part-time Nutrition Coordinator. I said I will call another friend of mine who is a Regional Manager at a Nursing Home. I figured he would know someone. He said sure, have the lady call me. I thanked him and said ok. As a follow-up, I called my friend, who inquired about the worker. I asked if Mr. Smith had called, and she said no, but she also stated, "I would rather have you." I said, "Oh No" my knees and my back hurt. Her response was, "You can do it!" So I conceded and started my new position on January 21, 2022.

Do you know, I feel better since getting out and back to work? God knows what you need!! So be encouraged today; God has a purpose for you. He has kept you so he could use you. If you need more information or prayer http://genevaonair.com

Geneva James Bio

Geneva James is the Director of Lift Him Up Ministries with 50 years of experience. Geneva specializes in ministering to those with alcohol and drug addiction. She is the media host of the Geneva Show, and she lives in Belleville, Michigan. She is from Phenix City, Alabama, where she attended South Girard High School. Geneva received a BA in Biblical Theology in 2017. Geneva is a powerful force in her ministry and uses her positive attitude, previous alcohol addiction experience, and faith to encourage others to work hard and succeed. Geneva is inspired daily by her children and her grandchildren. Geneva likes to cook, read, and write books in her free time.

Moving on by His Grace

STUCK NO MORE

Valila Wilson

Being confident of this very thing, that He which hath begun a good work in you will perform it until the day of Jesus Christ (Philippians 1:6).

Conversations

"You are never going to change. You don't have what it takes. You will start the work, but you will not finish. You are a master planner, but you suck at follow-through. Stop committing. You will not follow through and finish, therefore breaking your word. Come on, you know you. Be realistic when you make commitments. Do not promise anything. Just reside in the lane of noncommittal. Then, when the time comes, and you do not feel like it, you can back out without breaking your word or commitment. No one will count on you. This way, you are not disappointed, nor are you letting anyone down. You cannot even count on yourself. You will never achieve your hopes and dreams. You do not have what it takes to make them a reality. Why even dream, only to disappoint and let yourself down?"

What a horrible conversation! It is mean and devaluing. Who would say this to someone? These were my words to me. This was my belief and attitude. This was my perception of myself. I had believed it to be true because of my past failure and experiences. I felt like a fake and a fraud because I had so much potential but never seemed to be able to produce any real thing of value. Big dreams and hope tormented me. I knew I had a remarkable ability to do great things and positively impact others' lives. However, I got to the point where I stopped believing in myself. I began to give up on myself and lose hope. I knew there was greatness inside of me that others needed, but I didn't know how to overcome the flaws that held me from being who I knew I was created to be. I did not know how to break the cycle and get off the hamster wheel. I would find myself starting and stopping, starting and stopping. It was like my gears would get going, then something would cause them to get stuck and not correctly function. Sometimes it felt impossible to get them going again. This lifelong pattern had begun to take a toll on my soul. Finally, I found myself having another conversation.

"God, what is wrong with me? Why am I such a failure? I can't seem to get it together. I know you will do your part, but I am always falling short on my end. You have put so much greatness inside of me. Why can't I seem to be successful even in the little things in life, let alone the major things? Why do I struggle so much in life? Why does success seem to elude me? No matter how hard I try, I always miss the mark. I am always behind the eight-ball. Nothing I do is good enough. I have failed so many times I feel so worthless and insignificant. Why do I always start great, but never finish a thing? If I do manage to finish, I seem not to be able to maintain. I don't think I am ever going to change. I have been this way for so long, and I am only getting worse. I am getting older, and it seems things are getting harder. I am tired and don't have much fight left in me. God, I do not want this to be what I leave behind. God, I do not want to die without fulfilling your purpose and calling for my life, but this weight is heavy. The struggle is wearing me out, and I don't even have the energy for it all. God, please help me! I need you, or I will die unfulfilled. I will die without walking in my divine purpose and calling if you do not fix me. I want to be all that you created me to be. I want to be all you intended when you shaped me in my mother's womb. I need you, oh God almighty, and I need you now!"

At the beautiful age of 48, I found myself with a river of tears, a bleeding heart, and a broken back, desperately crying out to God in this conversation. These conversations expressed my brokenness stemming from all the unresolved trauma I had experienced. At about the age of 5, I was molested and abused by my god-sister, a young adult. From the age of 5 to 8, I remember, in addition to her, three other male family members who also took it upon themselves to violate me and steal my innocence. Meanwhile, at the age of 7, I had lost something else precious and significant. It had a profound impact on me. My once close-knit relationship and bond with my father had taken a turn. He became detached, distant, critical, judgmental, and unpleasant with me. Being a daddy's girl, I was devastated and heartbroken. I no longer felt special or valued, especially since our relationship never improved much as I grew up. The sad thing was that I didn't even know what I had done to cause his rejection and emotional abandonment. However, I now understand that unknowingly I had begun to give away his secrets to my mother. Because of this, he had chosen others over me, and

I was no longer Daddy's "Sweet Pea." I have realized that all this unresolved trauma had become toxic and was the root of my current anguish and turmoil.

I felt as though I was stuck in the quicksand of past failure, character defects, and flaws. However, the weight of this depression became more than I could bear. Despite all my knowledge, understanding, and ability, I could not fix Valila, and the slightest movement brought pain. So greatly pressed on all sides: shallow breaths were all I had. The light was fading, and the sand was doing its best to overtake me. So, I stopped fighting. I knew God was powerful. He was not the problem. I was! I did not know how to do my part. I certainly didn't know how to fix Valila. Would the quicksand have the victory? It certainly felt like it.

The Game Changers

If you can relate to what I have shared, then allow me over the following few pages to give you a gift. I want to encourage and empower you as I share a liberating process of victory and what changed the game for me. So just how did I break free from the quicksand? How did I begin walking in my purpose and calling? How did I get to the place of working on this project you are reading and another anthology lined up? How did I get to where my dreams and visions are becoming a reality? How did I get to where I am, becoming the person I envisioned God had created me to be? How did I come to a place of being stuck no more? My sisters and brothers, I have discovered the power of **"A, B, C."**

Together, they changed the game for me. They formed a fortified link chain that God used to pull me out and break free from the relentless crushing grip of what once was my pool of quicksand.

The Power of Accountability

Accountability, if done right, can be one of the most powerful forces in a person's life. It can be a catalyst that brings about great transformation. It enables you to grow at a faster pace or under more challenging circumstances. Accountability is a vital source of empowerment. I tell you, *The Power of Accountability* forever changed my life.

One way that accountability has been impactful for me is in its ability to serve as a scaffold. A scaffold is a temporary structure to support a work crew and materials. A scaffold provides the support needed in constructing, maintaining, and repairing buildings, bridges, and many other structures. You have seen them at construction sites or when someone is washing windows on a high-rise building. Often, the scaffold supports until what is being built or developed can support itself properly. This is one of the functions of healthy accountability. It provides support in those areas where our self-sufficiency is underdeveloped, and we are not yet able to stand and sustain. In other words, we need help because we have not developed a particular skill set, discipline, or fortitude required for an area. Accountability does a great job in this area.

The ability to serve as an anchor is another attribute that increases the power of accountability. Anchors hold water vessels in place and prevent them from drifting away. It remains to be a symbol of hope, strength, and steadfastness. This attribute is vital. Sometimes, because of the hustle and bustle of life, we can get distracted and lose our focus. Life's challenges and circumstances can often cause us to drift into dangerous and treacherous waters and possibly end up shipwrecked. We tend to drift without something to hold us steady and secure. We then realize we are hundreds of miles away from where we want or need to be. Even worse, we can find ourselves in undesirable situations. For these reasons, anchoring accountability is crucial for our continuous success.

The Power of Belief

I have heard it said, "You have to see it before you can see it." I know it can sound confusing. Let me explain. Everything that exists is created twice. It is envisioned first in the imagination and then manifested. Before it can be realized, it must first be imagined. Before anything can be produced in actuality, it must be an idea or a concept. The chair was conceived before it was created. The automobile was imagined first, then developed over time. Now we have a massive selection of cars to drive. Even you were thought of in the mind of God before you were in your mother's womb. You have to see (imagine, conceive) it before you see (produce, create, manifest, achieve, etc.) it. See it before you see it.

The question is, how does one get from imagination to realization? It is not enough to merely imagine a thing. Imagining or dreaming alone will not make it come to fruition or reality. So how do we get from *conceiving/ imagining* to *achieving/ manifesting*? Well, another element fits right in the middle of this process. It is very potent and is vital to this process. Without it, you will likely not make it across the finish line. Without it, dreams remain wishes, and success is elusive. It has a power all of its own. Without it, not much gets accomplished. "She believed she could, and she did." I am speaking of belief. Belief is the acceptance that something is true or exists. It is the trust, faith, or confidence in someone or something. Let me put a disclaimer. I am not talking about believing that you are a frog or a building or anything of that sort. No, that is not what I am referring to.

You may have heard of the concept, "Conceive →Believe→Achieve." Notice how "Believe" is dead smack in the middle. Many people imagine or dream but never achieve it. Many start, but the journey is short-lived. They fail to harness the true power of belief. I think "believe" is in the middle of "conceive" and "achieve" because it can propel you or restrict you. It can serve as a bridge or a gate. In other words, it is our belief that moves us forward or holds us back, or can empower us or hinder us. Belief will fuel our determination and tenacity. It will cause our endurance to be increased and fortify our strength. There is no achievement, accomplishment, or success without some level of belief, be it tiny or gigantic.

In college, I had read of an experiment that amazed me. Several once free sand fleas were conditioned to believe they had limits on how far they could jump because of a restricting lid covering the jar they had been placed in. When their circumstances had changed to total freedom, they still never jumped past the height of the lid. This conditioning even affected their offspring. Despite their offspring being born with the freedom to do as they wished from the start, the offspring never attempted to jump higher than the height of the lid that was on the jar their parents experienced.

Both the parent flea and their offspring had been conditioned by the limit of the lid that was imposed on them. Therefore, they accepted the lid as their reality of what was possible in any environment or situation. *The height of the lid had become their belief of reality.* The circumstance of the lid caused a mindset of limiting belief to develop and be passed on. Like the fleas in the experiment, this is how most of us develop our belief system.

Our belief has been conditioned by our experiences, circumstances, and environment. Here is the good news. If your past has caused you to develop limiting beliefs, *you do not have to keep them.* As a matter of fact, I had to get rid of my own limiting beliefs. Unlike the fleas in the experiment, our beliefs can be reconditioned to serve us positively. Limiting beliefs can be replaced with empowering beliefs. The essence of the power of belief is its ability to bring about transformation and bring us into a position for achievement. I encourage you to dream, imagine, envision, → Take the bridge of belief, and be empowered & propelled → to realize your hopes, dreams, and visions.

The Power of Choice

Choice may be listed last, but it is certainly not the least. As a matter of fact, nothing else would have mattered if I had not exercised the power of choice constantly throughout my process of getting unstuck. It was essential to the success of my process. The power of choice is about selecting from several possibilities and options. It can be considered a form of acceptance or approval. The choice factor is stronger than steel and should be highly valued. It is free and yet very precious. However, if made poorly, it could cost you considerably. It yields great power to build and the power to destroy. It will change your life for the better or worse. I have come to respect its great and mighty power. The great thing is everyone possesses the power of choice. We make choices every day, all day, and do not really give much thought to the energy we are accessing. It is essential to understand the magnitude of this power we have been given so freely. If used wisely, there can be much good to come. If used poorly and carelessly, it can cause massive destruction in our lives, communities, and the world. I know you have heard it said, "life is about choices." I believe this wholeheartedly. When I was first entering into entrepreneurship, I was taught a fundamental principle. I think it will bring much clarity. The principle of "The Slight Edge" says that little correct choices every day will eventually lead to you being on the upper curve of success. Quality, little, everyday decisions give you the slight edge of success over failure. The compound of one's quality, tiny, daily decisions will cause their success curve to shift and continue upward.

The power of choice gave durability to the other two links (accountability and belief) of God's power chain to pull me out of the quicksand. See, ultimately, I made a choice to live and not die. Each choice gave me the power to live and conquer that place of defeat, despair, and self-doubt. With each choice, I was empowered and grew stronger. I had to make many small, medium, and big choices daily to keep me on my upper curve of success and my path to victory. I didn't always make the best choice, but I chose to keep pushing toward the goal line.

Harnessing the Power

I have come to understand that my childhood trauma negatively conditioned me at an early age. The negative conditioning was continuously reinforced by various events and circumstances throughout my life. Here is the kicker, a lot of the situations, issues, and problems that had occurred were due to my choices and behavior. Choices and behaviors that stemmed from a coping and defense style that was forged from the fires of the traumas I had endured. I tell you, this was a vicious cycle I was stuck in, and it had me spiraling downward. The consequences of my choices and behaviors were becoming too much to bear. It was not only affecting me but those who were a part of my world.

It is critical for us to learn to harness the power of *accountability, belief, and choice* if we are to break free from the negative conditioning of our past and the vicious cycles that have become our norm. First, I had to learn how to harness the power of accountability, belief, and choice. I had to learn how to control and use their force and strength to produce the success I am meant to live. Once I did, I began to conquer what once conquered me. I started to operate in my authority. I began to dominate and take control. I began to grow exponentially and became a producer. How exactly did I break free from the quicksand of defeat, self-doubt, and despair? How did I harness this power? How do I continue to harness the power? When I look back in hindsight, I discovered five distinct principles I had to learn during this process. The power of "A, B, and C" was the driving force and was entrenched in executing these principles. I shared them with you in hopes that they will serve you as they have so greatly served me. Take note they are interrelated and interactive. These transformational principles will not only cause a positive shift in one's success curve, but if continuously practiced, they will produce sustainable success as well.

1. **Take ownership of your success**.
   Success is about purpose being accomplished. Success is determined by how well you accomplish what was set out to be done. When you set out to do something and achieve it, that is a success. That is a win, be it small or big.
   - Hold yourself accountable for your success. It doesn't matter what anyone else did or did not do. At the end of the day, it is your responsibility. If the ball was dropped by someone else, you must pick it up, do damage control, and carry it to completion.
   - Get rid of the limiting belief that you are not or cannot be successful because of others, circumstances, or even yourself.
   - Choose to take ownership and responsibility of your success! Make a choice not to allow anyone or anything to stop you. Do not even allow yourself to stop you!

2. **Believe That You are Possible**!
   I was blessed to hear a young lady by Tanisha Bowmen speak at a convention I attended. When someone tells her something

is impossible, she quickly changes it to "I Am Possible." She shared her story of trauma, struggle, challenges, and overcoming. She said she could have easily given up because she felt it was impossible. Instead, she decided not to give up and give it to God. She chose to believe what God said about her and trust the process.

- Hold yourself accountable for what you believe and say about yourself.
- Discover your limiting beliefs that say it is impossible and you cannot do it. Disable and discard all limiting beliefs!
- Choose to believe that you are possible. You are possible because a mighty God created you, and with Him, all things are possible. Choose to believe you are made with greatness, for greatness by greatness. You are possible!

3. **Stop Giving up on You and Quitting on God!**

I had come to realize that I frequently gave up on Valila. I became determined that No matter what, giving up simply was *not* an option! I decided not to allow my shortcomings and character defects to hold me back any longer. I chose to believe that God had begun a good work in me and would finish it. I set my mind to never give up on myself, my dreams, visions, or hopes.

Furthermore, I realized that to give up on myself was to quit on my Creator, who doesn't give up or quit on me. I was giving up on God, Jesus, and the Holy Spirit. I often quit on Jesus, my Lord and Savior, who didn't quit in the middle of His death for my sins. He finished His redeeming work. He died, was buried, defeated Satan on my behalf, was raised from the grave, and ascended to sit at the right hand of God. He finished, and so I chose to be a finisher as well.

- Build a healthy network of accountability and support to help you stay in the game and have sustainable success. Your network could consist of a sister or brotherhood, support groups, church, therapy, coaching, the faith-based community, accountability partner(s), mentor(s), etc.
- Get rid of your "lid" belief that only lets you go so high because of the uncomfortableness. Get rid of your "lid" belief that you don't have what it takes to accomplish your visions and dreams.
- Choose to embrace the truth of your possibility by never giving up on yourself. Choose not to quit on the Great God who created you with His greatness, for greatness.

4. Commit to Being Committed!

Without this, my freedom would have been fleeting. I would have been pulled under and succumbed to my pool of quicksand. This commitment broke the perceived power of my enemy and my toxic inner me. Neither they nor my pool of quicksand had any more power over me!

- Hold yourself accountable to the commitment of being committed to your purpose, calling, and success.

- Hold fast to the beliefs that will serve your commitment. Get rid of those beliefs that will cause you to waver in your commitment.
- Choose to commit to staying committed and not wavering. Choose to set your mind, be determined, and persevere against all odds. Choose to commit to yourself, your possibility, the God who created you, and those who need the greatness inside you. Choose to be committed to the process and your success.

5. Lock into Accountability and Stay Locked In!

For the power of accountability to be fully harnessed, a few crucial elements must appropriately be in place. There must be honesty and transparency. Permission of authority must be given, and responsibility of that authority has to be accepted. Mutual trust and respect must be established. It must be healthy for all participants, and it needs to be empowering. These elements have to exist at the core and throughout the process in order for one to truly lock into accountability and stay locked in. There is no success without some form of accountability, let alone sustainable success.

- Be willing and ready to give an honest and complete account within the process to your accountability network.
- Believe in the process. Believe in your accountability network and support system. Discard those beliefs that do not serve you and your process.

- Choose to embrace fully and committedly engage in accountability no matter how uncomfortable, painful, or challenging.

Move on by God's grace, harness the power, and be *stuck no more*!

Prayers

It is imperative that you understand that it was by the mercy and grace of God. It is Jesus' death and resurrection that made it possible for me to get unstuck. My relationship with Jesus as my Lord and Savior was my saving grace. I would have died without walking in my purpose and calling. I am moving on by God's grace.

You, too, can move on by God's grace. You can have your own story of being unstuck. God loves you just as much as He loves me. Jesus died for you to be delivered and free, just like He did for me. God desires to have a personal, intimate relationship with you. You are valuable and important to him. So much so that He sent Jesus to die for your sins. My sisters and brothers, understand that your sins (no matter how horrible you think or feel) are not an issue for God. You say, "But you don't know all that I have done." No, I sure don't. But, God sure does. Guess what? It doesn't matter! Come to God, ask Him for forgiveness. Ask Jesus to be your Lord and Savior.

If you have not received salvation and do not know Jesus as your Lord and Savior, please pray this prayer, or if you are not sure you are saved.

> *God, I come to you in the mighty name of Jesus Christ. I confess that Jesus is Lord. I believe in my heart that Jesus is your Son and died for my sins. I believe you raised Him from the dead. Thank you, Jesus, for being my Lord and Savior. God, please lead me to a church that you are pleased with, and I can be planted in so I will flourish in You. In Jesus' Name, Amen.*

Congratulations, my sister or brother! You have received salvation, and the angels in heaven are celebrating. My prayer is that you will be healed and made whole. I pray that you will be rooted and anchored in God. I pray that you will abound in the grace of God.

Please repeat these words if you have received salvation before but have walked away from Jesus being your Lord.

> *God, I come to you in the mighty name of Jesus Christ. I have confessed that Jesus is Lord. I believe that Jesus is your Son and died for my sins in my heart. I believe you raised Him from the dead. However, I have fallen away. I ask forgiveness for my sins, and I repent. Help me to turn away from my sin. God, I rededicate my life to you. I recommit to the Lordship of Jesus Christ. I submit to your Holy Spirit. In Jesus' Name, Amen*

Woo Whoo!! Welcome home! My prayer is that you will be healed and made whole. I pray that you will be rooted and anchored in God. I pray that you will abound in the grace of God.

If this chapter (Stuck No More) resonated with you even in the least little bit, please repeat this prayer.

Dear Lord, please help me no longer be overtaken by defeat, self-doubt, and despair. I want to be delivered and free. I want to thrive for the purpose you designed me. I want to be authentically me. I cannot do this without you. God, I need your grace for my process of getting unstuck. I need the redemptive power of Jesus Christ. I need your Holy Spirit to guide and teach me. I need your provision. Remove the scales from my eyes. Open my eyes of understanding. Help me to trust you with all my heart. Help me not to lean on my own understanding but acknowledge you in all my ways. Please direct my path. I need your wisdom and not my own. Teach me to turn away from evil out of respect, worship, and commitment for you, Lord. In Jesus's Name, Amen

Be encouraged, my sister and brother. You can be confident that God has started a good work in you. He will continue work to complete it. He will not give up on you. So do not give up on him or His process for your freedom.

This is my prayer for everyone that took the time to read this chapter:

That the Father of our Lord Jesus Christ would grant you, according to the riches of His glory, to be strengthened with might through His Spirit in the inner man, that Christ may dwell in your hearts through faith; that you, being rooted and grounded in love, may be able to comprehend with all the saints what *is* the width and length and depth and height to know the love of Christ which passes knowledge; that you may be filled with all the fullness of God. Now to Him who is able to do exceedingly abundantly above all that we ask or think, according to the power that works in us, to God *be* glory, forever and ever. Amen. (Ephesian 3:14 – 21, KJV)

Valila Wilson Bio

Valila Wilson is a dedicated, loving, and passionate mother of two adult sons. She is a lover of both the performing and fine arts. She is an enthusiast for knowledge, which she expresses through continuous learning, research, and exploration endeavors. Miss Wilson is a Transformational Success Empowerment Coach with over 30 years of leadership experience in ministry, business management, coaching, counseling, training, and entrepreneurship. Her roots run deep in her ancestry with a grandparent who trailblazed entrepreneurship in his community for African Americans. As a visionary, she has taken that foundation and built an empire of her own, including learning from some of the best in community and business leadership. Valila has a B.A. in Psychology; is a John Maxwell Certified speaker, coach, and trainer; is certified in business management with over three decades of experience; is ordained as an Evangelist and Minister; and is the founder of Essentially Beautiful Women's Ministry, Creations By Design, and Success Empowerment LLC. She's dedicated her life to helping others experience transformation and sustainable success through a strategic focus on personal, professional, and leadership development.

Contact Information:

valilawilson@tpds1.net
Instagram as Valila Wilson
Spotify: Podcast "Success Talk"
Facebook Pages: Success Empowerment LLC, Creations By Design, Essentially Beautiful 247

For the Website, please email at the above address

Moving on by His Grace

FROM TRAUMA TO GRACE
Karen Jaguar

"To appoint unto them that mourn in Zion, to give unto them beauty for ashes."
Isaiah 61:3 KJV

Living in Detroit in 1969 is where my true story began: a small family with a mom, dad, twin sister, and toddler brother. I witnessed my parents arguing and fighting regularly during my childhood, which made me nervous. Still, to this day, I do not like to be around argumentative people or rowdy situations. We were not a perfect family; my parents separated when I turned 11 years old, and my dad moved to the southwest side of Detroit. Mom stayed on the west side. At Christmas time, it seemed like a competition on who outdid each other buying our Christmas presents. Who brought us the best gift was a constant tug of war between them. Because of this, it became stressful for us. We only wanted our parents to get along. We loved them and did not want to choose sides on who brought the best gift.

We just needed to see love from them. Children need a loving environment. My parents did their best to provide for us. The only thing missing for me was experiencing a happy family life with both parents. After Christmas, when we turned 16, my sister and I asked our mom if we could move with our father to get to know him better. We were tired of her talking badly about him to us. We wanted to see how bad he was. She always spoke negatively about him. We needed to get to know him for ourselves. We were teenage girls needing daily interactions with our dad, and to our surprise, she allowed us to move with him. When I was 11 years old, my body began to develop early. Men were honking their car horns at me, and my mom was trying to protect me from neighborhood pimps. She noticed the attention I was receiving as I walked to the store, school, and home. My mom was a working, single mom. I felt terrible for her having to make sure her daughter was safe from the evil intents of men lurking after me. Why was this happening to me? I would tell myself I was a little girl with a grown-up body. I was 16, getting so much unwanted attention. That's why I believe she allowed us to move in with my dad. It was for our protection, and she needed a break from the madness. I understood my mom was still hurting from the separation and needed a break from everything.

My sister and I were premature babies at birth. When I was 13 years old, my mom told me I had a kidney condition that could cause problems during pregnancy. And it would be hard for me to have children. So, I thought I could never have kids and have many health issues growing up.

I knew it was hard on my mom. She carries a lot of bitterness and pain from separating from my dad, and she took it out on me because I looked like my dad. My sister and I are fraternal twins.

She looks like my mother. We were born on different days, May 17 was my birthday May 18 was my sister's birthday (because she was born after midnight). People thought we were just sisters, not twins.

In August, we moved to the southwest area of Detroit. We were excited to be in the new neighborhood and meeting new friends. And we were happy to get to know our dad better, up close. My dad worked the midnight shift at a steel plant, so he was here for us during the daytime before he went to work. He led an active life: playing pool, hunting, and fishing. He also was an outstanding tennis player. He tried to teach us how to play tennis, but we kept hitting the ball over the fence like we were playing baseball instead of tennis. He soon gave up teaching us tennis. Truthfully, we enjoyed watching him play against others rather than playing ourselves. I thought my dad was a professional tennis player.

When we were younger, my dad would take us to the more affluent neighborhoods. We looked at the beautiful mansions while he played jazz music on the radio. He had a 1957 Buick convertible. As we rode with the top down, our hair blowing in the wind, we had a wonderful time. My mom would never go with us when my dad asked her because she preferred to stay at home. Maybe this is one of the reasons they separated, because they enjoyed different things.

We were seeing the other sides of dad. He gave us chores to do daily, and on the weekends. We also had a curfew. We had to be home by 11 p.m. He would call at midnight to check if we were home.

My dad drove us to school on that first day of school. He let us off by the entrance. My sister and I walked together, heading to the entrance door. Several students came up to us, asking where were we from, and were we new to the neighborhood? They thought we were just sisters; they were surprised when we told them we were twins. The school gave us different classes. I headed out of the office to find my homeroom class, telling my sister where to meet me after school. As I walked down the hallway, boys tried to stop me by asking my name. I thought, "Oh no, not again." Finally, I made it to my room. As I was sitting down at my desk, several girls came up to me, handing me notes with their boyfriends' names on the paper, instructing me not to talk to them because they were already taken. This was my new welcome to my new school from them; their way of marking their territory. I quickly let them know I was not interested in their boyfriends.

One student, in particular, kept talking and following me around the school. He asked me for my phone number and to go to lunch with him or to the movies, every day. He would not stop pursuing me at school. Finally, I gave in. I told him to come to my house and ask my dad's permission to take me out. I gave him my address, and if my dad said yes, I would give him my house telephone number afterward. In addition, my twin would have to come on the date with us. I was thinking he would stop bothering me. With all those stipulations, he still came to my house and asked my dad if he could take me to the movies that Saturday afternoon?

My dad said yes, my sister came along, and my dad gave me extra money in case the date did not go well, we could take a cab home. He always believed in us having cash in case of emergencies. The boy told me he was happy to be with the new girl in the neighborhood. You are the talk of the school. The girls are jealous of you. You are pretty with a beautiful shape. I was so tired of being looked at that way. I was not happy about being the talk of the school. It made me feel like I was abnormal. Was I the only one being looked at like this? This made my teenage life miserable. Our date ended well, and we remained just friends only. I chose not to date anyone seriously at that time. I just wanted to do well with my school studies, enjoy bonding with my dad during the week, and visit my mom and brother on our weekends together. I was not looking for any drama, stalking, or gossip. I was enjoying myself and my surroundings.

After school, I saw a young guy that hung around the high school. He had graduated and he drove a purple Cadillac with a white convertible top. It was very noticeable. I saw him a lot at school, picking up a student after school and driving him home. The young man's parents owned a party store in the back of their house, and the kids in the neighborhood hung out there buying their goodies for their school lunchboxes. It was getting close to the weekend. I finished doing my homework; I had some daily chores to complete before the weekend fun began.

When I was five years old, my sister and I had roller skating lessons; I loved roller skating, so I planned to go roller skating on Saturday; that was my great escape for relaxation. Nobody bothered me. Everyone was there to roller skate. On Saturdays, my dad usually worked the midnight shift, but this particular day, he was called in early. So he dropped me off at the skating rink at noon. My sister wanted to go to the movies instead. My dad gave me money for food and cab fare home because he would not be able to pick me up. He would still be at work. It was important to him that my sister and I had cash on us for emergencies. He reminded us to be home before midnight; 11 pm exactly.

I was skating, going around the rink, skating fast as I passed people by, enjoying myself. I skated for hours until time got away from me. It was closing time, and it was getting dark outside. To make matters worse, I spent all my money on food, including my cab fare home. Now I would have to walk, which is a long 15 blocks away! I thought to myself how foolish I was. I should have at least saved my cab fare to get home. I walked down the busy street from the skating rink with my skates over my shoulder, and a car slowly pulls up beside me. The purple Cadillac I saw at the high school rolls down the passenger door window and asks if I need a ride. I hesitated for a minute. He said he would take me home. "Get in. It is dark out here." I only got in the car because I wanted to get home on time for my curfew, never knowing this would be the biggest mistake I could ever make. My life changed forever. That one decision getting in his vehicle changed my whole dynamic as a minor. You see, he did not take me straight home. Instead, drove me to an unknown location with abandoned houses. I was terrified. He parked the car. I thought about trying to open the door and run. He pulled me closer to him. I wanted to move him off me and struggled with him to keep my pants on. He overpowered me, and he forced himself on me and raped me. I thought if I just kept still, be motionless until he finished, it would be over. He finally took me home. It was way past my curfew time now. I ran out of the car as fast as I could to my front door. My sister heard me at the door. She saw the terror on my face when I entered the house. She knew something was wrong with me. She said, "Where have you been? When dad called at midnight, I had to pretend like I was you on the phone." I explained to her what had happened. I couldn't believe it myself. I was still shocked at how stupid and naive I was to get in a stranger's car, trusting him to take me straight home. I took a shower and lay on my bed, so embarrassed and afraid to tell anyone what happened to me. Only my sister knew my secret. As I lay there crying on my pillow, my sister hugged me all night. This traumatic event made me silent, wishing it was only a bad dream, hoping that when I woke up, it would be just a bad dream, but this was not a dream, my life as I knew it had changed forever.

I continued in school as if nothing had happened to me; no one knew my secret, but my sister. I blocked that Saturday night out of my memory. I continued going to school, doing my usual routine. On one of my weekend visits with my mother, she called me over and asked me if I was pregnant? I told her, no. Being pregnant was the last thing on my mind; I did not have regular periods, besides my mom had told me I would have difficulties having kids and could die from complications from childbirth. But my mom saw differently; she was convinced I was indeed pregnant. My mom called me saying she had made a doctor's appointment the next week. She told me to be sure to tell my dad, when he gets off from work that she was taking me to my doctor's appointment. I was still in denial, trying to block out that fateful night, pretending in my mind, that it never happened. It was like me living in the twilight zone. I was floating in space in my mind, not dealing with my actual reality ahead of me. The secret I had kept silent for so long, was now about to be revealed at the doctor's office. After the doctor examined me, he announced I was four months pregnant, I became hysterical, shaking and crying. I was thinking to myself, no more secret now. I continued to scream and cry out, as my mom kept trying to console me. But I kept thinking about what she told me when I was 13, I could die from complications at childbirth. I was really crying, because I was thinking I was pregnant, and I was going to die. As my mom drove me home, I told her everything that happened to me. She said she was going to call my dad when he got off from work, and she would be suggesting that I move back with her, because high schools did not allow pregnant students to attend classes. I felt so ashamed, I let my family down. It would look like it was my dad's fault, I got pregnant on his watch and care. It was all my fault, not my dad's. I should have never accepted the ride home from a stranger in the first place. I put myself into a situation that caused me to be overpowered, violated, and raped.

The following day was the worst day of my life; seeing my father's reaction to my mom's phone call the night before, during breakfast. He was reticent. As we headed to the car, I let my sister sit in the middle. I was too ashamed to sit next to him like I usually did. I had let him down, bringing shame to myself and my family. As he drove in silence to our school, I reached for the door. He told me I do not want you going to school, today. You might get hurt. Your mother told me you are pregnant. On the drive back home, I told him everything that happened when he dropped me off at the skating rink on that Saturday night. I described the color and make of the guy's car, and what a shame, I did not even know his real name, just a nickname they called him around the school. He was a stranger that I accepted a ride from. I had always been told that I was too I and trusting of people my age. This was a hard pill for me to swallow, but there was no undoing my situation. I was pregnant and had to go to the end of this pregnancy, no matter the future.

The side of town we lived in was a small community, so word about me dropping out of school due to pregnancy spread quickly. Although I moved back with my mom, a few of my friends from school asked my sister for my mom's phone number to keep in touch with me. To my surprise, a student who had a crush on me reached out to me by phone, claiming he wanted to marry me. I told him that it was a kind gesture, but that would not work in my situation. Meanwhile, my father got the name and phone number of the person who violated and raped me that Saturday night. There were arrangements made by my parents to speak with him. My mother was the one who did not believe my story, at first. She felt that I might have acted flirty and got in a sticky situation, way over my head to reverse. She wanted to hear what he had to say. He admitted what he had done to my mom. He told her that he would marry me and help raise the baby. He said he had a job and was very sorry for his actions and the pain he caused.

In the '50s and '60s, it was prevalent to say, "What's done in the house, stays in the house, because my mother was concerned about what the neighbors would think. So she agreed with him to marry me; the only problem is I did not want to marry him. He raped me. This man was a stranger to me. I did not love him.

But I knew why he wanted to marry me, he was thinking of himself, to keep from going to jail. It turns out he was in his 20's. I was a minor at only 16. My dad sided with me about not marrying him, so my mom decided the best thing to do for now,-was to put me in a home for unwed mothers. She did not want the neighbors to not find out that I was pregnant. She said since I did not want to marry him, the baby could be put up for adoption. This was the best solution because in her words, I was a baby having a baby. And there was no way out of this. I was too far gone to have an abortion. So, I was put into Lulabelle Home for unwed mothers, located at that time on the West Side of Detroit.

I delivered a healthy 7-pound baby boy, moved to my mom's house, and raised my son in church with the Lord's guidance; I never married his father, but I had enough forgiveness to allow him and his family to share in raising him.

I pray my story helps someone that has experienced something as traumatic as rape. If you have been raped or molested in any way, you know how traumatic this can be to anyone.

God Can Make Lemons Into Lemonade

There is no trauma, heartache, calamity, storm, or trial that God cannot bring you through. Often He will bring you out stronger, wiser, keeping you in your right mind, because God does make ways, out of no way. He will fight for you and raise you out of despair. God is unchangeable. He will never leave you or forsake you. He has an escape plan designed just for you. All you need to do is trust and believe that your God can and will do miraculous things if you allow him to be Lord of your life. I am a witness. Surrendering my will to God at 16, crying out for his help and guidance, he covered me with his supernatural power. What is that supernatural power? God's love. When you have God's love operating through you, that divine energy will cause you to survive being raped at 16. You must have forgiveness for the person that raped you because the unforgiveness will cause you to stay stuck in a cycle of pain. And keep you attached to your offender. You have to let go and move on with your life.

It was God's love that allowed me to keep my baby!! God's love is that powerful! Everything God made was made with love. It will be God's love to sustain you and keep you in perfect peace.

1. Please do not let bitterness set in your heart or mind. Instead, learn from it, and it will get better in time.

2. Trust God. He has a plan for your life. Find someone you trust to talk about it. For me, it was God. With his guidance, I held no bitterness for what happened to me.

3. Yes, I was able to walk in total forgiveness to the man who raped me, allowing him no jail time. However, despite the shame I brought to my family, I had to learn to also learn to forgive myself and move on. That is what you must do. It is necessary for your healing so bitterness does not set in your heart, hindering you from moving forward.

4. Move on, asking God to give you discernment and wisdom.

5. Talk to someone you trust. Be it a counselor, pastor, or trusted friend. It would help you to talk this out with someone. Not hold it in. You will see that the more you can share what happened to you, the more you are being delivered from the pain; forgiveness is a pathway for total

healing. It's essential to be wise, watch, and discern people's motives in your environment. You are trusting your inner voice inside you.

6. Be wise. With the internet these days you really must be wise in meeting people for the first time. Run background checks. Let friends know where you are and who you are meeting for the first time. Don't leave your drink unattended on a date with a new person, even having a friend with you or nearby to come to your aid if the situation seems unsafe.

7. Share your testimony. This is the key to being whole and living wisely, trusting God, and moving on with your life. This led me to meet an outstanding Apostle from Nigeria traveling with her. I was able to bring comfort and minister to a young girl named Esther brought to her orphanage who was raped at 11 years old by a pastor and encouraged her to forgive, and she has a beautiful life ahead of her

8. Get a journal and write out your thoughts. When it seems you can't find the words to talk to someone, you can always talk to God.

Trust in God. Just like I told Esther, I am saying to you trust God in every situation. Know that you can move on by His grace. Grace means divine favor, but it also means divine enablement. So, I pray for the favor of God and His enablement, not allowing rape to define you, and that you will become healed and whole.

Karen Jaguar Bio

Retired autoworker with Ford Motor Company. I was one of Ford's United Auto Workers' Singers. I sang at company events and UAW conferences and did company commercials.

After retiring, I began singing professionally, full-time. I also operate full-time in ministry in the office of Prophetess. I am a fashion designer; I make handmade custom accessories, purses, jewelry, and shoes by appointment. My business is Jaguar. Contact me at: msjag@msn.com

Moving on by His Grace

LINDA HUNT, VISIONARY

"The Anthology Doctor"

Bio

Linda Hunt is a prophetic gift to the body of Christ chosen to share her gift and talents in marketplace ministry. She has an extensive background in sales, marketing, and media. After years of journaling, she decided to use those journals to minister to women in need of healing and wholeness.

After writing her first book Amen Sister! she was inspired to bring other women along on the wonderful journey of writing as an anthology, and the title the "Anthology Doctor" was born. Her desire is to use the anthologies as a means for women to share their stories and open up streams of income and many doors of opportunities that will await them.

She has published 3 anthologies: Gathering the Fragments that Nothing will be Lost, Living and Loving Life Without Regrets, and Moving on by His Grace. In addition, she has helped many women tell their stories. Her desire is to have her next anthology exclusively for men.

Your next story could change your life and heal someone else!

www.ingramcontent.com/pod-product-compliance
Lightning Source LLC
Chambersburg PA
CBHW031636160426
43196CB00006B/442